Writhing Writing:
Moving Towards a Mad Poetics

Phil Smith

Weird Books for Weird People

Autonomous Press is an independent publisher focusing on works about neurodivergence, queerness, and the various ways they can intersect with other aspects of identity and lived experience.

ISBN-13: 9781-945955-10-5

Cover part by Jacqueline Pruder St. Antoine. She's a multitalented creative bringing a mad studies perspective into new space. Her full bio is in the back of this book, but you can also visit her website at: https://jstantoineblog.wordpress.com/.

To Roy George Bissonette and Gerald Cummings Pease, neither of whom made it past the 8th grade (Roy used to say "and it took me two times to do that!"), yet were extraordinary teachers who shaped the person I am today.

And, of course, to m. and s., for the reasons you both know.

Table of Contents

Acknowledgements

No book project is done in a vacuum. This one is no different.

I am deeply indebted to my wonderful friends at Autonomous Press, who proposed this thing, and made it happen. I've never acknowledged editors before. There's a reason for that. There's a reason why I'm acknowledging them now.

Jacquie St. Antoine—incredible artist, scholar, and madwoman—made the cover. It's awesome; she's awesome.

Jacquie, along with Kira Dallaire, Rachel Lewandowski, and Lzz Johnk, informed and shaped some of the content here. They are accomplices and co-conspirators of the highest order.

Many years ago, Corrine Glesne authorized me to play with words. Some of them appear here. She represents the kind of mentor that I try to be.

Norm Denzin, Shirley Steinberg, and Steve Taylor took risks to publish my work. When I grow up, I want to be like them.

The writing and thinking of Charles Bernstein, Norm Denzin, Carolyn Ellis, Patti Lather, Margaret Price, and Betty St. Pierre have shaped my own, sometimes implicitly and sometimes explicitly; sometimes in ways that can be identified, and sometimes not.

I owe much gratitude to the many attendees of the International Congress of Qualitative Inquiry, the Second City Conference of Disability and/in Education, and the Society for Disability Studies Annual Conference, over many years, for their infinite patience with my varied antics.

Formal recognition and thanks is owed to several publishers for allowing me to use my previous work here:

- an earlier version of "Inquiry Cantos: A Poetics of Disability" was published in 2001 in the journal *Mental Retardation* (now *Intellectual and Developmental Disability)* (*39,* 379-390) published by the AAMR, now the American Association of Intellectual and Developmental Disabilities.
- "Food Truck's Party Hat" was originally published in 1999 in *Qualitative Inquiry (5,* 244-261, doi: 10.1177/107780049900500204) by Sage Publications.

- "MAN.i.f.e.s.t.o.: Disrupting Taxonomies of D{evil}op{MENTAL} Dis{ability}" was originally published in 2001 in *Taboo: The Journal of Education and Culture* (5(1), 27-36) by Caddo Gap Press.

- "Split------ting the ROCK of {speci [ES]al} e.ducat.ion: FLOWers of lang[ue]age in >DIS<ability studIES" was originally published in 2006 in S. Danforth and S. Gabel (Eds.), *Vital Questions in Disability Studies in Education,* (pp. 31-58) by Peter Lang.

- "an ILL/ELLip(op)tical *po* – ETIC/EMIC/**Lemic**/litic *post*® uv ed DUCAT ion *re*cherché *re*pres©entation" was originally published in 2008 in *Qualitative Inquiry* (*14*, 706-722. doi: 10.1177/1077800408314353) by Sage Publications.

- "This Closet" was originally published in 2013 in P. Smith. (ed.). *Both sides of the table: Autoethnographies of educators learning and teaching with/in [dis]ability* (pp. 103-117) by Peter Lang.

- "BEyon|ce|D inclusion: Wud mite[ymose] be NEXTERATED X" was originally published in 2014 in D. Connor, J. Valle, and C. Hale (Eds.), *Practicing disability studies in education: Acting toward social change* (pp. 51-62) by Peter Lang.

- "~~[wo]mani**FEST**[ival][the big]0~~n*eu*roq*ue*er: nodes fer uh Grammuh C" was originally published in 2014 at the Neuroqueer blog (http://neuroqueer.blogspot.com/2014/04/womanifestivalthe-big0neuroqueer-nodes.html)

- "Contrab(l)ooshuns to ecojustice from a dis{co}/inter/ruptive per[trans]formative maaaad studies" was originally performed in 2016 at the Ecojustice and Activism Conference, Ypsilanti, MI.

- A somewhat different version of "An Immoderate Maaaaaadness: Why We're Pissed, What We're Gonna Do About It, and Why We're Not Asking Your Permission" was originally performed in 2016 at the Twelfth International Congress of Qualitative Inquiry, Urbana, IL, with Kira Dallaire, Lzz Johnk, Rachel Lewandowski, and Jacquie St. Antoine.

A Note

The chapters in this collection are generally arranged in the order in which I wrote them (the first chapter, "Inquiry Cantos," is put first, slightly out of chronological order, as it provides a kind of introduction for the work that follows). Read as such, they might be understood to represent the changes in my thinking and stylistic approaches over what is now approaching two decades. Together, they outline what I believe should be important directions for scholarship and its representation, in the interconnecting worlds of disability studies, education, and ethnography.

But then, I'm crazy as a motherfucker, so who knows.

Chapter 1: Inquiry Cantos: A Poetics of Disability

The Hmong have a phrase, "hais cuaj txub kaum txub," which means "to speak of all kinds of things." It is often used at the beginning of an oral narrative as a way of reminding the listeners that the world is full of things that may not seem to be connected but actually are, that you can miss a lot by sticking to the point, and that the storyteller is likely to be rather long-winded. (Fadiman, 1997, p. 12)

There is no thinking that does not wander, and any serious work should have etc. in its title and honestly state that it will not stick to the topic. (LeDoeuff, as cited in Bach, 1998, p. vii)

...it is time to do something that will be another path. (J. St. Antoine, personal communication, May 26, 2016)

♦　♦　♦

First Canto: Prologue

Summer at the university. A stuffy borrowed office on the fifth floor of the education building. Blazing sun outside, already hot at 10 a.m. In front of me, a blank computer screen. I sweat. I think of stories that want to be told, poems that want to written, about the lives of people with whom I've spent time, people who call themselves disabled. I think about how to describe the shape of what I am wondering about—this thing that my friends and colleagues and mentors and I call disability. I think about how to tell a story—a different kind of research story—to editors, reviewers, and (other) readers. About how to tell that story to myself. About how to tell that story about myself.

I play with a pencil. I look out the window. I open my thermos and pour a cup of coffee.

I look at those words, some written almost two decades ago (and others edited, or added), and laugh. It's coming on to summer again, and I live in a different state. My office—now my own, not borrowed from a dear, kind mentor—is on a piece of land I call, ridiculously, Flamingo Farm. The computer is a laptop. The thermos of coffee is in the next room, and I've not drunk from it because the words have, once again, caught me up. So I laugh at myself, get up and stretch—my joints ache more than they used to—and pour myself a cup. And stare at the words, as I have for 20 years—hell, I've been staring at words this way for going on 50 years now.

At the tail end of the 1990's, for about a year and a half, I worked on a qualitative research project in Vermont (P. Smith, 1999a). My intention then was to give voice to the words, actions, and stories of persons labeled as having developmental disabilities[1].

In listening to the words of these folks—people who became friends, colleagues, and co-conspirators over time—I started to get some beginning understanding about how they create and control supports, make decisions, and express power. I spent most of my time with people who call themselves self-advocates (described by professionals as individuals with developmental disabilities who speak for themselves)[2], all receiving a variety of supports from different non-profit agencies in Vermont, getting to know them and listening to their stories. I also talked with family members, direct support providers, and system administrators.

I began to feel that the stories that I had been given could not be written about in standardized academic language. It seemed to me that the stories themselves simply wouldn't stand for it. I tried writing them in traditional research forms, but they kept

---

[1] When considering terminology, I want to problematize the term *developmental disability* both in this text and in common use. The phrase developmental disability has roots in a medical model of disability, and privileges some (professionals) at the expense of others (people described as having a developmental disability). Although it is preferred by some self-advocates and family members as being less stigmatizing than other language, it remains caught in a web of professionalized power. The word *development* comes from the French *veloper,* which means to wrap up [Morris, 1975]. Coupled with the prefix *de-*, meaning reversal or undoing, the word can be read as a commentary on the way people with disabilities have been "unwrapped" from the center of cultural terrains, removed to the margin; and the prefix *dis-* in *disability* makes the same lingual move: it "is the semantic reincarnation of the split between disabled and nondisabled people in society" [Linton, 1998, p. 31].

[2] The notion of self-advocate is a complicated cultural metaphor. It implies another, principal form of advocacy, that is often paternalistic, of which self-advocacy is merely a (secondary, less important) variant [H. MacDuffie, personal communication, October 12, 2000]. When used by professionals, the term becomes a euphemism for "person with a developmental disability," and can become a way of taking power away from people. When claimed by people who call *themselves* self-advocates—often persons who have been labeled and oppressed in some way—it becomes a term with clear political tones, a way to claim disability as an identity, in the way identity is claimed by other oppressed groups. Although I want my usage to be more in alignment with that kind of claim, it can never be entirely so because I do not make a claim to being a self-advocate.

changing from those into other things, things they themselves wanted to be. I also realized that part of the reason these stories wanted to be written in alternative forms has to do with who *I* was (and am), and how I imagined (and imagine) the world to be. After a while, I stopped fighting them, realizing that I would need to write them in the form of fiction, narrative poems, and short stories.

I walk around the office, looking for fresh air in this warm room. Under the window is a dictionary lying open on a round wooden table (Oxford English Dictionary, 1971). At the bottom of the right column on the left page is a word: scherzando. *The dictionary tells me that scherzando is an Italian word used to describe to a performer the mood or tone of a musical passage. It tells the performer to be playful, literally to leap with joy. That is a good word, I think to myself. As a collaborative composer of music-stories, that word could give both me as performer-author and those unseen, imagined performer–readers, a hint about how to approach this text, how to co-write it with me.*

Back at the computer, I stare at the screen, thinking of another word: montage. *In the world of film, montage is the arrangement of seemingly disparate shots used to create new meanings, a greater whole. A filmic version of dialecticism, synergy. Montage is another good word to describe this text. Denzin (1995) said that "a written text becomes a montage (and a mise en scene), a meeting place where 'original' voices, their inscriptions (as transcribed texts), and the writer's interpretations come together" (p. 13). As a metaphoric filmmaker of words and stories, I would tell viewer–readers to think about the montage of stories as they watch this word-movie, putting together new meanings from separate pieces.*

When I wrote those words many years ago, I was a very different person than I am now. I have learned and grown and changed much in the intervening years. I now identify as disabled, mad, and neurodivergent[3]. I'm white, male, and middle-class. I've lived in the United States for most of my life, much of it in New England. I have a bunch of letters after my name, have worked in the broad field of education for almost all of my adult life, and describe myself as a disability and mad studies scholar.

---

[3] Mostly, here, I avoid "person-first language," using "disability-first" language instead. I do this, with other disabled people, "...to highlight their social identity as disabled people. It's a way for them to identify with and gain solidarity from a social group that gives them strength and power in the world... It also is a way for them to point toward the fact that disability is not something that is part of them, is not part of their mind or body, but is something imposed on them by society. In effect, they seek to highlight the fact that what disables them is not some part of themselves, but what society does to them" (Smith, 2014, p.5).

Among other jobs, I've worked as a factory worker, farm laborer, construction worker, daycare teacher, house cleaner, adventure program leader, and independent support broker. I was Executive Director of Vermont's Developmental Disabilities Council, and directed the Vermont Self-Determination Project. I'm a tenured full professor at a public regional university, as well as a published poet, playwright, novelist, visual artist, and a performance artist.

So. Here's a word-movie, a music-story. Interspersed throughout the text are clips of the stories I was given. Call the whole, montage. Call it scherzando. Call it fiction, poem, manifesto. Sing it.

◆   ◆   ◆

Second Canto: Song of Words

moron
imbecile
idiot
retard   mildly
         moderately
         severely
         profoundly   abnormal
                           deviant
                           pathological
                           incompetent   time-out
                                          antecedent
                                          modification
                                          consequence   nonverbal
                                                         low-functioning
                                                         vegetative
                                                         sheltered workshop
total care
group home
training school
supervised apartment   toileting

pre-vocational
telephone use
bed-making   IPP
                    ICF/MR
                    SIB
                    ABC   noncompliant
                                conduct disorder
                                oppositional   inclusion
                                                    seclusion intrusion
                                                    illusion collusion
                                                    exclusion delusion

◆   ◆   ◆

Third Canto: Words and Knowledge About Developmental Disability

. . . the way things are said is more important than the possession of truths. (Rorty, 1979, p. 359)

As a poet and photographer, beginning with work I started in the 1970's, I've been interested in and in alignment with visual, written, and performance art that was decidedly and firmly on the fringes—work that many found incomprehensible, strange, and without meaning. As I began to work with and advocate for disabled people in the 1990's, I started to see a disconnect between the way I thought about the world, and the way that professionals and academics understood society, culture, and our place in it. As I read and learned and explored, though, I started to find a few scholars that looked at ways in which what has come to be called post-modernity might offer new ways of thinking and understanding (Danforth,1997; Danforth & Navarro, 1998; Peter, 2000; Ronai, 1997; S. Taylor, 2000). These ideas and debates led me to rethink what I had taken for granted about the work that I might do as a writer, artist, and scholar. I started to read farther afield, to see how this and other illegitimate thinking might be applied. I began to think about words and how they construct knowledge.

I began to realize that we draw pictures in our minds of the worlds around us, through the use of maps. We draw mental maps of even the most elusive and ephemeral qualities around us. Mostly, these maps aren't put down or drawn up on paper, or at least the kind of paper at which most people look. Some philosophers and poets describe these maps using words—but philosophers and poets aren't folks that the silent majority of Western people pay much attention to in their daily lives.

McKnight (1995) said that "each of us has a map of the social world in our mind" (p. 161). Maps can be about not only geophysical worlds, but also about the many worlds of relationships and ideas. Sometimes we draw these maps graphically, but more often we use words to describe them. Using this metaphor of cartography, I saw that some progressive, critical educators, researchers, and other cultural workers began to draw disability as a social construction instead of an objective reality (some examples include Biklen, 1998; Bogdan, 1992; Bogdan & Taylor, 1994; Danforth & Navarro, 1998; Ferguson, 1994; Furney, Glesne, Kervick, Pillai, & Smith, 1998; Kliewer, 1998; Kliewer & Drake, 1998; Neath, 1997; S. Taylor, 1996; Trent, 1994). Some took a further step, portraying disability as a metaphor (Biklen, 1998, 1999; Bogdan & Taylor, 1994), almost (but not quite) in the same way that poets and other artists think about metaphor.

I came to recognize that the way people use language—the words we make and the order we put them in—tells us about how we understand the world (Warren, 1997). Understanding words about disability as culturally created metaphors gives us opportunities for figuring out who creates disability, where it is created, who is supported by it, who benefits from it, and how to deconstruct it. This, it struck me, was a terrain that it would be useful for disabled people to explore, in order to begin to unpack ableism[4] in our culture.

I also saw that the production of knowledge— and I thought specifically about the knowledge of disability—and the language used to re-produce it, is compartmentalized by artificial, academic boundaries (Ellis & Bochner, 1996; Sibley, 1995). Some words can be used only by certain people, and as a result of speaking them, the importance and validity of those persons is accentuated (A. Smith, 1997). Different words, spoken by Others[5], cannot be

---

[4] Ableism is an ideology, a set of ideas (and practices) that impact, and reflect, how we think about the world—in this case, disability. In Western culture, "ableism, as an ideology, creates, supports, and permits the oppression, persecution, and discrimination of people who are said to have disabilities, by people who believe that they do not have disabilities..." (Smith & Salles, 2014, p. 23).

[5] *Other* is a complicated word, one I do not want to simplify with a direct and linear definition. Glesne [1999] used it as a postmodern alternative to words such as "research participants, respondents, interviewees, and researched" [p. xii]. Guba and Lincoln [1994] defined it parenthetically in the plural as "nonmainstream lives" [p. 106]. Jones and Ball [1995], in discussing the work of Michel Foucault, suggested that the *Other* "comes in many forms: the alien, the strange, the criminal, the incomprehensible, the pathological, and most particularly the insane. . . . Otherness is the antithesis of reason and epistemology seeks to subject it to reason. This subjection takes the form of scientific inquiry and diagnosis of the irrational subject, whether it be the criminal, the insane, the diseased, the child, or the woman"

heard or spoken at all.

Danforth (1997) pointed out some of the ways that rhetoric employed in understanding developmental disabilities serves this purpose, effectively excluding what he called "non-science voices" (p. 105). Fields of "applied" knowledge in which this rhetoric is employed have held positions of enormous power over the lives of people labeled as having disabilities for a very long time (Donnellan & Leary, 1995; Heshusius, 1995; Kliewer, 1998; Linton, 1998; Linton, Mello, & O'Neill, 1995; Sleeter, 1995; Wendell, 1996).

It occurred to me that words are often used to create the territorialization of knowledge, especially when they are jargonate (a word that means precisely itself: jargon words). This language protects professional understandings in the field of rehabilitation and disability services from infection by viral outbreaks of critical thought, especially when spoken by disabled people. In addition, "compartmentalized knowledge, kept within secure boundaries, gives power and authority to those who peddle it" (Sibley, 1995, p. 122). Disability researchers and practitioners are kept safe in their positions and roles by explicitly *not* exploring terrains outside the boundaries of their field; and people with disabilities, with their families, are kept securely outside the boundaries of communities of which they seek to be a part.

An important tool used by those guarding knowledge borders is the creation of idea taxonomies and hierarchies of knowledge. Some knowledge—or more precisely, some knowledge expression—is deemed of greater value than other knowledge expressions by those in the dominant social group (white, cis-het, middle or upper class, college-educated): "other knowledge is considered 'lower' if expressed in different idioms, for example, the writing of journalists but also writing in unconventional academic styles" (Sibley, 1995, p. 122). Knowledge presented in the conventional written forms and codes of modernist positivist research, forms typically used in representing academic disability research, is given greater cultural value than knowledge presented in other forms, such as poetry, drama, fiction, and the like.

Bernstein (1997), a poet, noted that there is a "growing discrepancy between our most advanced theories and institutionally encoded proscriptions on our writing and teaching practices" (paragraph 2). Even as postmodernist ideas and disability studies approaches gain traction, academic scholarship continues to be represented in conventional, professionalized formats. Bernstein called this discrepancy "frame lock" and said that it is a result of

---

[p. 47]. I like all of these thoughts, and I like the thought that a definition of the word is inherently [or at least ideally] multivocal, and multisensed.

"ideational mimesis," "an often repressed epistemological positivism about the representation of ideas" (paragraph 6). By this, he meant that traditional ways of expressing scientific knowledge control how that knowledge is talked about. Bernstein pointed out that in the same ways that some of what has been considered foundational to modernist thought—notions of transparency and neutrality—has been critiqued, so too has the notion that writing can essentially duplicate those qualities been confronted and disproved.

With Bernstein (1997) and Linton (1998), among others, I began to wonder how to undo frame lock in research and scholarship with and by and for disabled people. I quickly realized that to do so would entail a new kind of writing, a new kind of thinking, a new kind of knowledge-making. I wanted to find ways to move out of the Age of Enlightenment into the Age of Entanglement, in which the work that I engaged in was not merely cross- or trans- or inter-disciplinary, but anti-disciplinary (Oxman, 2016). I wanted to do something different, to engage in "...thinking the world differently" (St. Pierre, 2013, p. 652).

♦   ♦   ♦

Fourth Canto: Lemmings

He's sick of being treated like an animal
He says
no one listens
He feels like everyone is telling him
to stop hoping
He feels empty, empty
He says to quit calling him dumb
He is not a child
He wants to be smart
to feel hopeful
Hope is necessary
Hope is essential

He feels like a lemming, he says
lemmings follow
lemmings empty him of hope

He says he wants to make his own decisions
He says he wants to be in charge of his life
He says he wants to do what he wants
He says he wants to get his own place
He says he wants to get out of here

"let me go"

◆   ◆   ◆

Fifth Canto: Crisis and Release

Today, the modernist, pragmatic method of knowing is under assault. The very methods of knowing are themselves no longer certain. Modernism's pragmatism falters at that precise moment when the phobia for truth confronts the truth of the simulacrum; the truth that says there is no truth. Suppose, then, that nothing is any longer certain, except uncertainty. If this is so, then science and ethnography are no longer certain, only two among many discourses about reality (Denzin, 1995, p. 16).

Progress is a myth (Danforth, 1997). Objectivity turns out to be an illusion; it always was. In fact, "the Real... never existed at all" (St. Pierre, 2013, p. 650). For some, this shifting epistemology is a crisis. What was once stable is now always on the move. Nothing can be taken for granted.

Perhaps, though, this is a crisis only because of metaphor. Epistemology—the study of knowledge, what it is and how it works—is supposed to be a "foundation": unmoving, concrete, stable, never-changing. When I lived in a sagging farmhouse on a hill in Vermont, I had a different understanding of foundations: they are more like boats, floating in an ocean of soil. The foundation under my old house shifted and creaked every winter, weighed down from above by several feet of snow and pushed up from below by inevitable frost. The porch out front heaved up every February, making it hard to open the kitchen door. A wall near my woodstove had a long crack in it because it moved a little differently than the others. No matter how they're built, foundations shift and move, whether by frost or tectonic action.

Maybe it would be better to think of epistemology as the small sailboat I used to go to when I escaped to Maine, sliding up and down the waves. If I tied the boat up on a beach in a spot with a long tide fall, I would be apt to find the boat high and dry the next day. As a researcher standing on the boat of inquiry, if I try to stand with my legs straight and unbending, as I do on dry land, I will fall over. I need sea legs. I need to follow the motion of the water underneath me, my knees working as shock absorbers.

If I think of epistemology as a boat, then the postmodern turn looks less like a crisis and more like a release. I am no longer tied up to the dock. I can set sail and let the current, tide, and wind take me along, seeing many new things from many new vantage points.

This strikes me as an especially advantageous way of thinking about inquiry into disability. The postmodern moment gives us an opportunity to explore how and why and for whom we have created and inscribed disability. It gives me an opportunity not just to include disabled people in my work, but for them to direct and control that research, to have choices in their supports, to be emancipated participants in their communities, and to gain power in their lives. And it gives me an opportunity to look at my own life experience as a source for "data."

Griffin (1997), a feminist, marked language as being in a similar position. The correspondence theory of truth—the idea that words describe and denote a separate, objective reality—is no longer valid. As a result, the place that words and language hold in our lives can be understood as problematic, even tragic. On the other hand, Griffin said,

> "The dependency of words on each other, and finally the inability of language to determine truth, makes language dependent on other forms of knowledge, and other modes of existence; it signals an end to the only partly submerged goal of language to master reality, and it also sets language free from that goal. Language can then be explored as another mode of existence. Real in itself. A different territory." (p. 218)

The validity of alternative research forms in disability studies and research is not made to refer to the "reality" that they are thought to describe, but rather to the words that they speak. Words become the essence of research, acting as real, not just metaphoric, blood (P. Smith, 1997).

◆   ◆   ◆

Sixth Canto: John's Song

It's hard to imagine John as a boy.
His hair is white now
and there are brown age spots on the backs of his hands.
He grew up at Langdon Training School, mostly,
spent his life there.
He lived only a little while with his parents
and then they couldn't take care of him anymore.
The family doctor said one day, as a lot of them did back then
Well, you know, you should send him off to Langdon.
He'll be much happier there, with his own kind.
So he went as a young boy
and that was his whole life.
That's all he's known, the back wards.
Course he's out now, been out for four, five years.

That doctor maybe, or some other doctor at Langdon
called John the name
he'd have the rest of his life,
made the word stickwith that special glue they use.
Severely mentally retardedthey called him;
resulting from encephalopathythey said—
a three dollar word in a five cent suit
that means he's different from the normals.

When they called John that name
it stuck to his white skin
like gum to the underside of a schoolroom desk
over time turning hard and dark
so brittle and clinging so tight you'd have to chisel it off
if somebody had wanted to do that.
It's become part of the molecular structure of his skin
etched in underneath the short smooth hair

that grows on the inside of his wrist
where you can't see it unless you know where to look.
Or maybe it's better to think of it
as a tattoo of numbers and letters
that tells those who know a little history
about where he's been kept.

When they gave him that name
they figured it meant something, they figured it was real
part of John's actual being
real like a cup of coffee you had for breakfast
real like a mourning dove out in your dooryard
real like a weight hung around your neck
so heavy it pulls your head down to the ground
you can't ever stand up
always hunched over
looking at ants or
blades of grass
or stones
if you can ever even open your eyes wide enough
to see through the pain of the heaviness.

◆   ◆   ◆

Seventh Canto: Stories and Poems

*It is a way of making these lives available to others in a form that differs both
from the extended narratives of heroic biography or case history on the one hand
and the lost individuality of the survey on the other.* (Bateson, 1989, p. 16)

Over the last couple of decades, as I read as widely as I could about research and
scholarship in disability studies, mad studies, and neurodiversity, I started to feel
uncomfortable about the way much of it—especially that written by professionals—
presented itself as getting to some kind of singular truth, getting to what is real, about people

and the world they live in. It began to be clear to me that much of this research was devoted to simplifying, to reducing complexity in hopes of increasing understanding (P. Smith, 1999c). For those making inquiries into disability, the impact of such research representation is the making of knowledge that captures only part of a human experience. The potential understanding any of us have of the idea of disability is limited if only one way of representing and creating knowledge is used and given value.

This felt dangerous to me, because the lives of disabled people and their allies that I was coming to know were anything but simple, unable and unwilling to be coded in numeric or other terms. Instead, I yearned for a way of representing research— knowledge-making—that could focus on and exemplify in the writing itself the complexity and sometimes conflicting natures of people I was meeting. I wanted to get to what some researchers have called a "plural text" (Ellis & Bochner, 1996, p. 15), one that would represent, in both form and content, the "subjects" (perhaps *co-creators* is a better term) of inquiry not as singular things but as multiply faceted, ever-changing, active, and responsive beings-that-don't-stand-still. And so it was that I started to imagine what the representation of inquiry into the lives of disabled people (including myself) would look like if it were, in poetic terms, "a polyphonic, heteroglossic, multigenre construction" (Rose, 1993, p. 218).

I also began to understand that a life and its written representation can never be the same (Glesne, 1999). In terms of my own research, the descriptions that I wrote of the lives of disabled people could never be the same as their actual lived experiences. Unavoidably, whatever I or other researchers say about another person or experience or attribute always passes through the filter of our own experience, picking up other flavors as it goes. These flavors are not abhorred, at least by some researchers, but celebrated. Like the multiple tastes within wine, coffee, or chocolate, many simultaneous flavors enhance experience rather than detract from it.

Qualitative researchers have begun to move across the ideological divide from objectivity to subjectivity. Some disability studies and postmodern researchers, seeking a way out of what is seen as a simplifying binary of objectivity/subjectivity, look to avoid this dualism by assuming multiple subjectivities. One anonymous reviewer, responding to an earlier version of this text (and so this text itself becomes multiple, nesting within responses of reviewers and the counter-texts of myself as author), noted poetically that "the call of subjectivities (plural, positioned, multi-voiced, contingent, inconstant) is the hope of pluralistic community and idiosyncratic individuality, of a particularity, of experiences, of hope, of suffering" (Anonymous reviewer, personal communication, August 22, 2000). This described, for me, a vision of an inclusive community of researchers, disabled people, activists, family members, and others—a community that finds troubling the power ensconced in disability research journals and texts that deny access to the writing and reading of disabled people.

I was also troubled by the place of truth in disability and other research and, ultimately, about the difference between fiction and nonfiction. From a positivist perspective, writing that does not make some claim to truth (as does most modernist research), that sees instead a world of multiple, even conflicting, truths (as is true for postmodernist perspectives), must be inherently untrue, must portray a kind of fiction. And fiction—that which is made up—was less equal, less important, than truth-telling so-called non-fiction.

This didn't make sense to me. As a writer, a maker of fiction and poems and stories and plays, I knew that fiction had much truth to share about the world. Besides, as another maker of fiction wrote, "Important wasn't the point. Things didn't have rank" (Le Guin, 1991, p. 36).

I came to a stance more like that of popular novelist King (1989), one of whose characters, a writer, talks about "the almost unconscious act of fictionalizing one's own life" and that "the overflow of make-believe into one's own life seemed to be an almost unavoidable effect of storytelling" (p. 271). Another novelist, Banks, wrote that

> ...there is an osmosis from fiction to reality, a constant contamination which
> distorts the truth behind both and fuzzes the telling distinctions in life itself, categorizing
> real situations and feelings by a set of rules largely culled from the most hoary fictional
> clichés, the most familiar and received nonsense (Banks, 1989, p. 6.20).

The idea that fiction had no truth in it, and that truth had no fiction in it, just didn't make sense to me. Nor could I any longer accept that truth was a single thing—it was multiple, poly, constructed.

Acceptance of a perspective in which there are multiple truths, in which I expressed multiple subjectivities, meant that the line in my research between fiction and nonfiction, truth and non-truth, became a slippery hog, refusing to hold still, refusing to be held. By calling my research-writing fiction, I knew I would confuse some researchers and practitioners. To call it otherwise, though, would seem false to what I thought postmodern disabilities studies research could be.

I began to recognize that all of what we call research—whether critical, interpretivist, positivist, or postmodern—was in some sense a kind of story, a tale, a way to organize our thinking in order to describe it to others. Put another way, philosopher C. Taylor (1989) said that "we grasp our lives in a narrative" (p. 47). The narratives that make sense to us are stories and experiences with which we can empathize. Stories of research that do not make sense to us are ones that do not fit within our frame for understanding the world. A postmodern story about research that calls all research a kind of fiction, a story, will seem oxymoronic to some, yet as metaphors for research and knowledge-making, they have equivalent, if conflicting, truth value.

Stories and poems, rather than denying the multiple, complex, and chaotic natures of human existence, assert them, place them at the center (Kociatkiewicz & Kostera, 1999). In poems and stories, the relationship between writer and written, researcher and researched, knower and known is a relationship that is never taken for granted. This quality of not being taken for granted was one that I searched for in my representation of the lives of self-advocates. The philosopher Gadamer (1997) described that quality in his criticism of the poetry of Celan:

> I do not believe one should think of a You in these poems only when they speak of a You, or that one should think of the poet only when he says "I." Both seem wrong to me. Might not an I say You to itself? And who is I? I is never simply the poet. It is always also the reader. (p. 118)

Poems are about relations, connections, what is between, what Gadamer (1997) called "the event of the word" (p. 120), not the poles of artist and audience. Poems imply audience; the act of being a poet necessitates the act of being a reader. That relationship, and the relationship between myself and Others, were ones with which I was most interested.

Gadamer (1997) also noted that "all that matters is what the poem actually says, not what its author intended and perhaps did not know how to say" (p. 68). This frees readers to create new meanings, some perhaps in conflict, understanding that "poetics aims at inviting the reader toward reading, interpreting and co-authoring the text" (Kociatkiewicz & Kostera, 1999, p. 42).

Poets have begun to recognize that "the binary opposition between poetry and science is an arbitrary one" (Wersher-Henry, 2000), in the same way that disability studies theorists have critiqued the separation between science and nonscience (Linton, 1998). These boundaries are disappearing in the same way that fog lifts out of spruce woods to reveal the brilliant blue sky of a clear autumn day. Some researchers have begun to outline a poetics of inquiry (Sandelowski, 1994). Such a poetics has the potential for exploring the cultural construction and reification of disability, of understanding of how we as members of our society inscribe disability on the bodyminds and lives of others. Inquiry into the lives of disabled people takes on at least two tasks: explicating cultural metaphors and creating new ones. The process of creating new metaphors of disability deconstructs old ones, unpacking their social baggage for a new journey.

Lather (1995), a researcher who worked with women living with HIV/AIDS, talked about wanting in her work to "question taxonomies" (p. 58). Her intent, I think, was to explode the way science creates hierarchies of knowledge, hierarchies of people, and hierarchies of privilege. I saw an affinity between this and my own work with disabled people, for I had accepted that it was essential that the stories I described should, as critical theorist Giroux (1997) said,

> acknowledge and critically interrogate how the colonizing of differences by dominant groups is expressed and sustained through representations: in which Others are seen as deficit, in which the humanity of the Others is either cynically posited as problematic or ruthlessly denied. (p. 156)

This, then, calls for not just a poetics of inquiry, but also a poetics of politics (Sultana, 1995). Some in the fields of inquiry about disability separate ideology and science (Mulick, 1990). They believe that the study of reality "... involves the belief that the world, a thing, can be accurately, objectively recorded, painted, photographed, transcribed, performed" (Denzin, 2011, p. 159).

I had come to believe the opposite—that ideology and science are inseparable, and that research is never value-free, nor should it be (Maguire, 1996; P. Smith, 1999b). Research is an inherently overt political act, should be understood as such, and should be evaluated (at least in part) as being so. Rather than denying that it has no point of view, researchers investigating disability should be explicit about its value.

Further, I realized that "all knowledge is local, all truth is partial... No truth can make another truth untrue. All knowledge is a part of the whole knowledge" (LeGuin, 1995, p. 140). This recognition was not nihilist, or relativist, at least in any negative sense. Instead, I understood that there is value in local and partial knowledge—that there is value in many knowledges, and many ways of knowing. The knowledge of trees—not the knowledge about trees held by humans, but the knowledge that trees themselves have about themselves and the world—this knowledge is something that might inform all beings, animate or inanimate. They're not separate, or separable, anyway: "we are not separate from the world. Being in every sense is entangled, connected, indefinite, impersonal, shifting into different multiplicities and assemblages" (St. Pierre, 2013, p. 653).

Increasingly, qualitative research is being represented in alternative textual formats, as poetry (Glesne, 1997; Glesne et al., 1998; P. Smith, 1999d; Weems, 2000), as readers' theater (Donmoyer & Yennie-Donmoyer, 1995), as fiction (Stewart, 1989), and in texts that intersect multiple practices (Jipson & Paley, 1997; Lather & Smithie, 1997).

I also found examples of alternative representations of the lives of disabled people persons in short stories (Angrosino, 1998) and poetry (Blatt, 1970, 1973, 1981). There are autoethnographies about disability (Ronai,1997; Smith, 2013); and there are representations of people with disabilities in pop music, including the Beatles (1967), Mary Chapin Carpenter (1994), and R.E.M. (1988).

Still other works that might be considered alternative, in that they would not otherwise be accepted as research texts, are autobiographical narratives or memoirs written (sometimes with the support of others) by disabled people, including Johnson (1999), Crossley and MacDonald (1984), Sienkiewicz-Mercer and Kaplan (1989), and Williams (1992, 1994, 1996). Also not otherwise accepted as research texts are the autobiographical poems of Josephson (1997) or Sellin (1995).

These other voices, not accorded the privilege and status provided to academic researchers, are perhaps more pointed and critical because they have nothing to lose:

> I'm a sock in the eye with gnarled fist
> I'm a French kiss with cleft tongue
> I'm orthopedic shoes sewn on a last of your fears
> I am not one of the differently abled-
> I'm an epitaph for a million imperfect babies left untreated
> I'm an icon carved from bones in a mass grave at Tiergarten, Germany
> I'm withered legs hidden with a blanket (Wade, 1995, p. 30)

This is the kind of poem, telling a story that is "pissed-off" and not afraid to admit it, that needs to be authorized and privileged as authentic, legitimate research (P. Smith, 2000).

◆   ◆   ◆

Eighth Canto: Who's In Charge?

"Ah, my dear," sighed Mr. Obscenity, sitting upright amid the damp rumpled
sheets and patting Miss Flatface on the thigh. "I'm afraid you've had it. One must never
think that no other life than this is possible. All other lives are imaginable, possible, even
probable." (Sontag, 1978, p. 62)

So, with others, I began to look around at what has been called the crisis of representation,
to find new ways of understanding the lives of labeled Others through alternative textual
practices. Sitting in that borrowed office, analyzing the interviews and observations I had
done, I realized that I needed to move beyond typical analytic and writing practice in
disability research and scholarship. I would need to develop and create text acts outside of
typical academic prose: poetry, fiction, drama, even performance and visual arts. I also began
to recognize that the analysis of the stories that I had been told would be a bit
unconventional.

For I had come to realize, with Richardson (1994), that the process of writing itself is a
form of inquiry, a way to understand the world. The analytical process would be not just
through a conventional procedure of pulling together themes from a variety of stories, a
variety of data trails. It would also be a process of writing down those stories; the process itself
of writing them down, of telling those stories, would also be a way of understanding them. As
St. Pierre notes, "...writing is not mere writing nor is its work merely linguistic but always
already exquisitely ontological and material" (2013, p. 652).

I would not be able to know what the stories meant until I had written them; they would
not be until they had been written.

The title of Merwin's (1993) poem "Writing Lives," proclaims the inscription of the lives
of people through research texts:

Out of a life it is done
and without ever knowing
how things will turn out

or what a life is for that matter
any life at all
the leaf in the sunlight the voice in the day

the author in the words

and the invisible
words themselves
in whose lives we appear
and learn to speak
until what is said seems
to be almost everything
that can be known
one way with the words is to tell
the lives of others
using the distance as a lens

and another way
is when there is no distance
so that water
is looking at water . . . (p. 9)

Given what I have come to know and believe about research, this seems as useful an epistemological wondering as any written by academic social scientists and disability researchers. Some researchers try to understand through an objective stance, forgetting the ways that the "distance" provided by objectivity is metaphoric, forgetting that such distance is not value-neutral. The alternative described by Merwin is partly about the importance and celebration of subjectivities ("water looking at water"). It is also partly about the difficulty at looking at subjectivities (how can water look at itself, especially when it's invisible, even to itself? And even what we use to describe multiple subjectivities, words, invisibly inscribe!), partly about seeing the Self in the Other (and the place between, at which "there is no distance"), perhaps even something about rejecting the negative value sometimes placed on "going native." This poem is not a finished statement of epistemology; it is a question, a work always in progress.

Poet Codrescu (1986) reminded me that "'the word,' William Burroughs said, 'is a virus'" (p. 194). Words infect us with culture (Dawkins, 1991). I wanted my research representations of the lives of disabled people (including my own) to be an infectious cultural agent that would begin to change how people think and act and understand what they call disability. This viral infection would work in a way similar to the way one sometimes experiences a sense of contradiction while looking at a work of art, the way the contradiction between the multiple meanings present in the work of art (of whatever kind) creates new ways of thinking about and being critical of the world (Palermo, 1999). This is the kind of text that, in the language of Lather (1995), "fosters brooding" (p. 48).

Some have expressed misgivings, warned about the kind of illegitimate narratives that I began to write and that appear in this text: "One who fails to tap into the language of modern science may be unconvincing" (Danforth, 1997, p. 105). I discovered in writing these cantos, though, that I didn't have much choice in the matter. I wasn't exactly in charge here. Authorial autonomy? A ridiculous notion. I just followed behind the stories, picking up the pieces.

◆   ◆   ◆

Ninth Canto: Epilogue

Since I wrote the first version of this chapter many years ago, my writing style, and my thinking about it, has continued to change and evolve. My work has been increasingly opposed to the representation of knowledge and exploration that is academified (L. Johnk, personal communication, May 21, 2016). My writing has become increasingly performative, both in the writing of it, and in the for-the-page and oral presentation of it. At conferences, I've performed, with others, scripted, poly-vocal, intentionally-en-jumbled, crosstalking, choral, mad, glossolalic verbal-magic, soundfield explosions of almost-sense. Versions for the page are increasingly enjambed, twisted, disorderly, concretist, entangled, anti-linear, cripped, echolalic, rhizomatic wonders of liminal written prestidigitation.

This book represents a kind of genealogy of my writhing writing. Dance to it. Shout it out from the tops of mountains and from dingy basement apartments. Sing it. Sing it loud. Reeeeeeeeeal loud. And laugh while yer doin' it.

CUT TO borrowed office. Haggard researcher sits in front of a computer, thinking and staring. On the table to his right is a book, Bogdan and Taylor's (1994) The Social Meaning of Mental Retardation, *page 77, to which he glances.*

SLOW ZOOM IN on the open book until it more than fills the screen. Words are highlighted as we read along:

"The word 'retarded' is a word."

The camera TILTS UP to the computer screen, on which an internet web page is displayed (Chopin, 2000). Again, the words are highlighted:

It is impossible, one cannot continue with the all powerful Word, the Word that reigns over all. One cannot continue to admit it to every house, and listen to it everywhere describe us... The Word... has permitted life to lie... it creates the inaccurate SIGNIFICATION . . . The Word is useful no more...

SLOW ZOOM OUT to full shot of office. Researcher slowly disappears from the room; computer slowly disappears; books, plants, desk all slowly disappear until nothing is left but an empty room. CAMERA PULLS BACK through window, still slowly ZOOMING OUT, to shot of the building on a pleasant summer day, PULLING BACK to helicopter shot of campus with many small people walking around, PULLING BACK to shot of the entire city, and finally, FADE TO BLACK.

◆   ◆   ◆

Ridiculously, Sorceress Sources[6]

Angrosino, M. (1998). *Opportunity house: Ethnographic stories of mental retardation.* Walnut Creek, CA: AltaMira Press.

Bach, H. (1998). *A visual narrative concerning curriculum, girls, photography, etc.* Edmonton, Canada: Qual Institute Press.

Bateson, M. (1989). *Composing a life.* New York: Plume.

Beatles (1967). Fool on the hill. On *Magical mystery tour* [CD]. Capital Records.

Bernstein, C. (1997). *Frame lock.* [Online]. Available at: http://epc.buffalo.edu/authors/bernstein/essays/frame-lock.html

Biklen, D. (1998). Foreword. In C. Kliewer, *Schooling children with Down syndrome: Toward an understanding of possibility* (pp. ix–xiii). New York: Teacher's College Press.

Biklen, D. (1999, May). *Lessons from the 20th century.* Keynote address at the Moving On: Facilitated Communication in the 21st Century Conference, Portland, ME.

Blatt, B. (1970). *Exodus from pandemonium: Human abuse and a reformation of public policy.* Boston: Allyn & Bacon.

Blatt, B. (1973). *Souls in extremis: An anthology on victims and victimizers.* Boston: Allyn & Bacon.

Blatt, B. (1981). *In and out of mental retardation: Essays on educability, disability, and human policy.* Baltimore: University Park Press.

Bogdan, R. (1992). A 'simple' farmer accused of murder: Community acceptance and the meaning of deviance. *Disability, Handicap & Society, 7,* 303–320.

Bogdan, R., & Taylor, S. (1994). *The social meaning of mental retardation: Two life stories.* New York: Teachers College Press.

Carpenter, M. (1994). John Doe no. 24. On *Stones in the Road* [CD]. Sony Music.

Chopin, H. (2000). Why I am the author of sound poetry and free poetry [Online]. Available at: http://www.ubu.com/papers/chopin.html

Codrescu, A. (1986). *A craving for swan.* Columbus: Ohio State University Press.

Crossley, R., & MacDonald, A. (1984). *Annie's coming out.* Victoria, Australia: Penguin Books.

Danforth, S. (1997). On what basis hope? Modern progress and postmodern possibilities. *Mental Retardation, 35,* 93–106.

Danforth, S. (2000). What can the field of developmental disabilities learn from Michel

---

[6] J. St. Antoine, personal communication, May 21, 2016.

Foucault? *Mental Retardation, 38,* 364–369.

Danforth, S., & Navarro, V. (1998). Speech acts: Sampling the social construction of mental retardation in everyday life. *Mental Retardation, 36,* 31–43.

Dawkins, R. (1991). *Viruses of the mind* [Online]. Available at: *http://www.spacelab.net/catalj/virus.htm*

Denzin, N. (1995). The experiential text and the limits of visual understanding. *Educational Theory, 45,* 7–18.

Denzin, N. (2011). *Custer on canvas: Representing Indians, memory, and violence in the New West.* Walnut Creek, CA: Left Coast Press.

Donmoyer, R., & Yennie-Donmoyer, J. (1995). Data as drama: Reflections on the use of readers theater as a mode of qualitative data display. *Qualitative Inquiry, 1,* 402–428.

Donnellan, A., & Leary, M. (1995). *Movement differences and diversity in autism/mental retardation: Appreciating and accommodating people with communication and behavior challenges.* Madison, WI: DRI Press.

Ellis, C., & Bochner, A. (1996). Introduction: Talking over ethnography. In C. Ellis & A. Bochner (Eds.), *Composing ethnography: Alternative forms of qualitative writing* (pp. 13–45). Walnut Creek, CA: AltaMira Press.

Fadiman, A. (1997). *The spirit catches you and you fall down: A Hmong child, her American doctors, and the collision of two cultures.* New York: Farrar, Straus & Giroux.

Ferguson, P. (1994). Introduction to "On the politics and sociology of stupidity in our society." *Mental Retardation, 32,* 151.

Furney, K., Glesne, C., Kervick, C., Pillai, M., & Smith, P. (1998, November). *The social construction of disability: A scripted conversation.* Paper presented at the annual meeting of the American Educational Studies Association, Philadelphia.

Gadamer, H.-G. (1997). *Gadamer on Celan: "Who am I and who are you?" and other essays* (R. Heinemann & B. Krajewski, Trans. and Eds.). Albany: SUNY Press.

Gelb, S. (2000). "Be cruel!" Dare we take Foucault seriously? *Mental Retardation, 38,* 369–372.

Giroux, H. (1997). *Pedagogy and the politics of hope: Theory, culture, and schooling.* Boulder, CO: Westview Press.

Glesne, C. (1997). That rare feeling: Re-presenting research through poetic transcription. *Qualitative Inquiry, 3,* 202–221.

Glesne, C. (1999). *Becoming qualitative researchers: An introduction* (2nd ed.). New York: Longman.

Glesne, C., Leyva, C., Pillai, M., Smith, P., Taylor, L., & Weems, M. (1998, November). *Poet as activist: Second annual poetry reading by AESA poets and educators.* Presented at the meeting of the American Educational Studies Association, Philadelphia.

Griffin, S. (1997). Ecofeminism and meaning. In K. Warren (Ed.), *Ecofeminism: Women, culture, nature* (pp. 213–226). Bloomington: Indiana University Press.

Guba, E., & Lincoln, Y. (1994). Competing paradigms in qualitative research. In N. Denzin & Y. Lincoln (Eds.), *Handbook of qualitative research* (pp. 105–117). Thousand Oaks, CA: Sage.

Heshusius, L. (1995). Holism and special education: There is no substitute for real life purposes and processes. In T. Skrtic (Ed.), *Disability and democracy: Reconstructing (special) education for postmodernity* (pp. 166–189). New York: Teachers College Press.

Hillis, D. (2016). The Enlightenment is dead, long live the Entanglement. *Journal of Design and Science.* Available: http://jods.mitpress.mit.edu/pub/enlightenment-to-entanglement

Jipson, J., & Paley, N. (1997). *Daredevil research: Re-creating analytic practice.* New York: Lang.

Johnson, R. (with K. Williams). (1999). *Lost in a desert world: An autobiography.* Plymouth Meeting, PA: Speaking for Ourselves.

Jones, D., & Ball, S. (1995). Michael Foucault and the discourse of education. In P. McLaren & J. Giarelli (Eds.), *Critical theory and educational research* (pp. 39–52). Albany: State University of New York Press.

Josephson, G. (1997). *Bus girl.* Cambridge, MA: Brookline Books.

Kennedy, M. (2000). Opening the doors of opportunity for the year 2000 and beyond. *Mental Retardation, 38,* 373–374.

King, S. (1989). *The dark half.* New York: Penguin Books.

Kliewer, C. (1998). *Schooling children with Down syndrome: Toward an understanding of possibility.* New York: Teachers College Press.

Kliewer, C., & Drake, S. (1998). Disability, eugenics and the current ideology of segregation: A modern moral tale. *Disability & Society, 13,* 95–111.

Kociatkiewicz, J., & Kostera, M. (1999). The anthropology of empty spaces. *Qualitative Sociology, 22,* 37–50.

Lather, P. (1995). The validity of angels: Interpretive and textual strategies in researching the lives of women with HIV/AIDS. *Qualitative Inquiry, 1,* 41–68.

Lather, P., & Smithies, C. (1997). *Troubling the angels: Women living with HIV/AIDS.* Boulder CO: Westview Press.

Le Guin, U. (1991). *Searoad: Chronicles of Klatsand.* NY: Harper Collins Publishers.

Linton, S. (1998). *Claiming disability: Knowledge and identity.* New York: New York University Press.

Linton, S., Mello, S., & O'Neill, J. (1995). Disability studies: Expanding the parameters of diversity. *Radical Teacher, 47,* 4–10.

Maguire, P. (1996). Considering more feminist participatory research: What's congruency got to do with it? *Qualitative Inquiry, 2,* 106–118.

McKnight, J. (1995). *The careless society: Community and its counterfeits.* New York: Basic Books.

Merwin, W. S. (1993). *Travels.* New York: Knopf.

Morris, W. (Ed.). *American heritage dictionary of the English language.* (1975). New York: American Heritage.

Mulick, J. (1990). The ideology and science of punishment in mental retardation. *American Journal on Mental Retardation, 95,* 142–156.

Neath, J. (1997). Social causes of impairment, disability, and abuse: A feminist perspective. *Journal of Disability Policy Studies, 8,* 195–230. *Oxford English Dictionary.* (1971). New York: Oxford University Press.

Oxman, N. (2016). Age of entanglement. *Journal of Design and Science.* Available: http://jods.mitpress.mit.edu/pub/AgeOfEntanglement

Palermo, J. (1999). "I'm not lying, this is not a pipe": Foucault and Magritte on the art of critical pedagogy. *Philosophy of Education, 1994* [Online.]. Available: *https://www.csudh.edu/ dearhabermas/palermo.htm*

Peter, D. (2000). Dynamics of discourse: A case study illuminating power relations in mental retardation. *Mental Retardation, 38,* 354–362.

R.E.M. (1988). The wrong child. On *Green* [CD]. Warner Brothers.

Richardson, L. (1994). Writing: A method of inquiry. In N. Denzin & Y. Lincoln (Eds.), *Handbook of qualitative research* (pp. 516–529). Thousand Oaks, CA: Sage.

Ronai, C. R. (1997). On loving and hating my mentally retarded mother. *Mental Retardation, 35,* 417–432.

Rose, D. (1993). Ethnography as a form of life: The written word and the work of the world. In P. Benson (Ed.), *Anthropology and literature* (pp. 192–224). Urbana: University of

Illinois Press.

Rorty, R. (1979). *Philosophy and the mirror of nature.* Princeton, NJ: Princeton University Press.

Sandelowski, M. (1994). The proof is in the pottery: Toward a poetic for qualitative inquiry. J. Morse (Ed.), *Critical issues in qualitative research methods* (pp. 46–63). Thousand Oaks, CA: Sage.

Sellin, B. (1995). *I don't want to be inside me anymore: Messages from an autistic mind.* New York: Basic Books.

Sibley, D. (1995). *Geographies of exclusion: Society and difference in the west.* New York: Routledge.

Sienkiewicz-Mercer, R., & Kaplan, S. (1989). *I raise my eyes to say yes.* Boston: Houghton-Mifflin.

Sleeter, C. (1995). Radical structuralist perspectives on the creation and use of learning disabilities. In T. Skrtic (Ed.), *Disability & democracy: Reconstructing (special) education for postmodernity* (pp. 153–165). New York: Teachers College Press.

Smith, A. (1997). Ecofeminism through an anticolonial framework. In K. Warren (Ed.), *Ecofeminism: Women, culture, nature* (p. 21–37). Bloomington: Indiana University Press.

Smith, P. (1997). *Not words: Blood* [Online]. Available at: *http://www.flash.net/suffrn/oldjour. html/*

Smith, P. (1999a). "I know how to do": Choice, control, and power in the lives of people with developmental disabilities. *Dissertation Abstracts International, 60* (11) A, 3965 (University Microfilms No. 9951862).

Smith, P. (1999b). Ideology, politics, and science in understanding developmental disabilities. *Mental Retardation, 37,* 71–72.

Smith, P. (1999c). Drawing new maps: A radical cartography of developmental disabilities. *Review of Educational Research, 69,* 117–144.

Smith, P. (1999d). Food truck's party hat. *Qualitative Inquiry, 5,* 244–261.

Smith, P. (2000). *MAN.i.f.e.s.t.o.: A POETICS of d(evil)op[mental] dis{ability}.* Paper presented at Desegregating Disability Studies: An Interdisciplinary Conference, Syracuse, NY.

Smith, P. (ed.) (2013). *Both sides of the table: Autoethnographies of educators learning and teaching with/in [dis]ability.* New York: Peter Lang.

Smith, P. (2014). What is disability? In P. Smith (Ed.), *Disability and diversity: An introduction* (p. 3-7). Dubuque, IA: Kendall-Hunt.

Smith, P. & Salles, R. (2014). Defining ableism. In P. Smith (Ed.), *Disability and diversity: An introduction* (p. 23-26). Dubuque, IA: Kendall-Hunt.

Sontag, S. (1978). *I, etcetera.* New York: Vintage Books.

Stewart, J. (1989). *Drinkers, drummers, and decent folk: Ethnographic narratives of village Trinidad.* Albany: State University of New York Press.

St. Pierre, E. (2013). The posts continue: becoming. *International Journal of Qualitative Studies in Education, 26*(6), 646-657. DOI: 10.1080/09518398.2013.788754

Sultana, R. (1995). Ethnography and the politics of absence. In P. McLaren & J. Giarelli (Eds.), *Critical theory and educational research* (pp. 113–125). Albany: State University of New York Press.

Taylor, C. (1989). *Sources of the self: The making of the modern identity.* Cambridge: Harvard University Press.

Taylor, S. (1996). Disability studies and mental retardation. *Disability Studies Quarterly, 16*(3), 4–13.

Taylor, S. (2000). Introduction to two perspectives on Foucault and postmodernism. *Mental Retardation, 38,* 363.

Trent, J. (1994). *Inventing the feeble mind: A history of mental retardation in the United States.* Berkeley: University of California Press.

Wade, C. (1995). I am not one of the. *Radical Teacher, 47,* 30.

Warren, K. (1997). Taking empirical data seriously: An ecofeminist philosophical perspective. In K. Warren (Ed.), *Ecofeminism: Women, culture, nature* (pp. 3–20). Bloomington: Indiana University Press.

Weems, M. (2000). Windows. *Qualitative Inquiry, 6,* 152–163.

Wendell, S. (1996). *The rejected body: Feminist philosophical reflections on disability.* New York: Routledge.

Wersher-Henry, D. (2000). *Noise in the channel, or I really don't have any paper: An antifesto* [Online]. Available at: *http://www.ubu.com/papers/ol/dwh.html*

Williams, D. (1992). *Nobody nowhere*: *The extraordinary autobiography of an autistic.* New York: Times Books.

Williams, D. (1994). *Somebody somewhere: Breaking free from the world of autism.* New York: Times Books.

Williams, D. (1996). *Like color to the blind.* New York: Bantam Books.

Chapter 2: Food Truck's Party Hat

1.
He looks me square in the face, square as a man can whose head doesn't
ever stop bobbing and weaving, swooping and diving.
His head is a butterfly looking for nectar in a field of flowers,
a swallow in the darkening sky searching out mosquitoes,
a surfer climbing up and down green waves under a setting sun.
 Food Truck's blue eyes look for mine
while his smile and almost-white hair slide and weave and float in the air
in front of me.

Boy use jug
he says, and grins, and puts the frayed corner of his jacket collar into his mouth. He takes it
out again, his head moving in a complex knot I can't untie. His face loops around the room,
eyes caught by the Christmas cactus hanging from a hook in front of the window, his head
continuing to glide, a river slipping over water-smoothed boulders. He goes to it faster than a
blink, at 65, still quick; has to be, afraid someone would stop him probably, if they could.

He sticks one wrinkled finger into the soil in the pot, puts it carefully to his mouth, tastes it.
Tests it, in fact, a human soil analyzer. He checks every
plant basket
sand bucket
flower garden
he sees, checking the soil for sweetness, maybe mineral content, acidity level, the proper
balance of organic material, I don't know, but he tastes them all, every time, over and over.
Maybe he can tell something about the weather from the taste, or who was there last, or how
long the plant will live or what kinds of bugs burrow underneath. Most people think he's an
old whacked retard, probably, putting his dirt-smeared finger into his mouth. To me he's a
connoisseur, a critic, a scholar of soil. I imagine he's got all the ground in New England, half
the United States maybe, cataloged and chronicled, logged into some
unknown

neurological
taxonomy   ;
of dirt.
We all eat a peck before we die, they say, and I reckon he's got his more than covered.

2.
He looks at me again, grinning again
his head moving, his whole body, really, in
constant
literal |
actual
motion, he never entirely stops, some part of him always racing
beyond the rest of us
tappingswinginggliding always
in continuous seamless
never-ending can't-make-it-stop not-even-in-sleep motion.
Boy use jug
he says, and laughs, eyebrows raised, a question.

No one knows, now, how Food Truck came to that phrase
or to the name he calls himself.
He lived for over 40 years
behind brick walls
at Langdon Training School,
where they used to lock up all the people they called
morons
imbeciles
epileptics
retards.

Boy use jug he says,
and pulls his thumbnail on his upper teeth to make the clicking noise he likes. Out of
Langdon now 4 or 5 years, he says that every time he has to go to the toilet, instead of telling

people he wants to pee (or instead of going to use the bathroom on his own without telling anybody first, like most of the rest of us).

I imagine Food Truck's seen it all, living at Langdon all those years, though he doesn't talk about it. But when we sit together at Burger King, eating lunch, he with his cheeseburger, fries, Coke (no ice), apple pie—the same thing, every Friday noon—me across the table watching carefully to see he doesn't shove the whole burger into his mouth at once –
I look at the scars
on the back of his gentle thin-skinned old-man hands
wonder how they got there
afraid I don't want to know.

3.

I met a woman once who grew up at Langdon too, except she didn't live in the dorms. She lived in a big white house right at the top of the hill, with nice carpets on the floors and pretty blue irises on the wallpaper in the dining room, and they had steak every Thursday night for supper. Her father was the superintendent, and she told me what it was like to be in that place:

I grew up on the grounds of the Training School
I knew I was different from them.
I remember riding down hills past dorms
riding as fast as I could
that's the dorm where the screams came from
that's the scariest one
they're going to be yelling at you as you ride by on your bike
go as fast as you can
I hope nothing happens to my bike chain.

We would go to the J and K buildings, which had the difficult people
looking through the locked doors, through the window
seeing naked people
seeing a room, the day room,
with a TV way up in a corner, in a cage,

the people not engaged in anything
seeing someone just drooling, looking up
the men running around naked,
the attendants demanding:
"Get over here."
"Stop that."
"Don't do this."
And that institutional smell.

The enclosed porch area, which was just tar, pavement
and people were not lying on it, naked.
The bathroom area,
all those big trough tubs in a row
hoses attached to them.
Gee, I have a nice bathroom.

And I lingered, peering into the window,
just taking one last look.
The loneliness –
that's it,
that's their life
and really not knowing anything about it.

I'm pretty sure Food Truck lived in J building for a while.

4.
Food Truck doesn't call a lot of things by the names most of us know.
He's got his own way of naming things
His own name, of course, isn't Food Truck, it's Barry.
But he never calls himself Barry.
I guess at Langdon, they didn't make food on all the wards
they had a truck go around to different buildings with the meals.
Barry, he's a big eater, got a hollow leg they say,
I can imagine the attendants saying to him,

Here comes your food truck, Barry.

When Food Truck sees me sometimes,
he says *Don't Touch the Man's Glasses.*
That's his name for me
when the glasses on my face
keep him from seeing into my heart.
Sometimes he reaches for them and takes them from my head
and gives them back to me,
hands them to me, a gift
and I tell him politely I would prefer that he not do that
and we look at each other
and he walks away
and I feel like hell.

A former case manager he calls Little Bo Peep.
I don't know why, her name's Maureen.
His guardian is hung with the name Mississippi,
which rhymes with what she calls herself,
and she always smiles when she hears Food Truck call her that.

5.
Food Truck says again
Boy use jug,
his head a locomotive so heavy and loaded with inertia
it takes a mile for it to stop moving.
I grin, and say
C'mon Barry; ya gotta do what ya gotta do.
He and I head down the hallway
walking slowly at Food Truck's wandering pace
weaving through barriers only he can see
his eyes corn brooms constantly sweeping the air.
We stop at the water fountain as we always do
he leans over as he always does, and carefully tastes the water

just like always, to be sure it's still there, I guess.
Testing the water like he tests the soil
a walking Environmental Protection Agency
keeping us all safe from pollution.

6.
We go into the men's room, lights off.
I fumble for the switch
while Food Truck, who knows his way around every public restroom
this side of the state,
slides as surely as a key into a lock
over to the far stall and opens the door.
He always uses that stall first,
 and then the other stall
and then the first again, just like opening your eyes
when you wake up, it's so predictable.
Why does he do that, the same thing in the same way every day
over and over, over
and over and over again?

Like he tells the old woman he sees every Friday
when we go to Burger King,
the one with most of her teeth missing
who works in the kitchen but comes out halfway
through our meal just as regular as if you'd turned her on with a switch,
after she asks him
kidding
whether he's been to the library lately
and he always grins saying, *Kicked out of the library.*
And he and I and this old woman
with her Burger King hat a little crooked and a
splotch of grease on her pants laugh
to think about what it must have been like
the day when Food Truck was asked to leave the library

probably for making too much noise.
The same story
in the same voice
most of it not told.

 Thinking of that question
 why he says the same things
 and does the same things,
 I wonder what it was like another day
sitting with his brother on the front porch
with the gray floor except for the one board still pale wood
they had replaced last summer, waiting
for them to put all the bags in the old car.
They were taking the old car because it had just snowed
the first snow of the season,
and they figured it would get up the hill better than the new one
they would probably keep in the barn anyway
until spring came.
And then the old man told him to get in the car and
his brother rubbed his knuckles hard on top of his head
which he hated so he yelled and
they picked him up and put him in the back seat and
he sat crying and
he looked out the back window
at the house with its roof painted white by the snow
although it was starting to melt
and drip off and
then he couldn't see the house anymore and
he never saw it again though he didn't know it then
riding in the back seat of the old car
with his brother sitting next to him.

If he had known
would it have been different

would he have gotten into the car,
or would he have hung onto the porch post
so tight and hard
they would have had to pull his fingers from it
the way you pull potatoes from the earth with your hands,
fingernails aching, him screaming
and then hitting and
the old man yelling now and
his brother going to one side to stand by the maple
with his hands in his pockets looking at the ground
with his eyes hot and red but no tears and
mother sitting in the car crying
like she had been already the last few days. And

the next day him waking up in bed
with all the others waking up
at the same time because
someone was shouting beds
all jammed together tight when
do we eat when
do we sleep why
don't we have pancakes on Saturday night anymore
with syrup
and who's that
he wasn't here last week
and the way the old man used to laugh
sometimes
and then they never come anymore and then
it becomes so long ago so far away it must have been a dream.
A dream.
And besides we watch TV inside the cage thing
"Jeopardy" is on in the afternoon.

 So what do you do?

What do you do?
You try to tell them
don't change the channel
you want to watch "Jeopardy"
but they don't understand the words
and one of them likes to watch "MASH" instead so
they watch that
and you start to yell and
pull down your pants and say *party hat* and
then the staff run and they hold you down on the floor
so hard for a long time
and your face hurts on the concrete and
you cry and no one wipes your face when
it's over when
they let you up
and then you go to the place where they won't let you watch "Jeopardy"
or anything at all
for a really long time.

Have I said he lived there
for 40 years?
I should say that, so you'll know,
so you'll remember.

You do the same things day after day after day
to keep it from being a dream
so you won't forget who you are
or if it's winter again
to be sure no one goes away or comes back or gets old.
You do the same things day after day after day
to keep your thoughts in your mind in your body so they don't leak
out to spill on the floor like that one time when

someone pulled their toenail off

and the blood made a puddle under the chair.
You do the same things day after day after day
to keep the world spinning on its axis to keep the food in your mouth
to keep "Jeopardy" coming on every afternoon still
on even if they won't let you watch it.
You do the same things day after day after day
so you don't have to feel bad again
the way you did, not the day when you went away
but the day you realized you weren't ever going back home again. That's
the day
you feel bad.

Although there's another day that is pretty bad too
bad in a different way
a funny way
a way you don't want to think about much
the day when it doesn't matter anymore that you're not going back
because where you are
is home now.
Going back stops being something
you think about, there is only just right here

going to the bathroom in one stall
then over to the other one and then
back to the first one
and drinking the water and tasting the dirt and
touching my glasses because they shine too much
I can't see into his heart
and sitting at the big table not the little one
at Dunkin' Donuts and make sure you buy a juice
and the woman gives you six donut holes
every day
and
she always

smiles.

7.

Food Truck and I walk back down the hall.
Something's bothering him today but I don't know what.
I don't know either if walking
is the best word to describe what we do,
but it's the only one I can think of:
we float for a stretch
stop short
spin
laugh
speak to a friend
swim on again
find the water fountain
test its freshness and clarity
move along.
Food Truck teaches me
every time I go with him that a walk down the hall
is a safari into a jungle just out of my sight.
He dodges enormous, elephantine dust motes
blowing in the hall's river of air.
He gives a wide berth to the tiger-roar
of conversation from offices on either side.
Other people like red fire ants
march down the carpet towards us,
and he lifts his feet
carefully and gently to move around them,
holding my arm for safety.
He looks at me and laughs and says
Pain in the ass
and I don't know if he means the ants or
me or him
or some remembered story I will never hear.

Food Truck pulls his shirt collar up to his lips,
sucks it in,
then takes it out again.
He does this so many times every day,
his collar is frayed,
torn,
always damp with mouthjuice.
He does this so many times every day,
I can almost always smell
the saliva on his shirt.
Something's bothering Food Truck today but I don't know
what he's pulled the glasses off my
nose twice already this morning and
he's never done that before. On the way over
he asked to ride in the back of the car which means he's not feeling safe enough to
keep his hands off the wheel like the time he
almost made me have an accident. I ask
Food Truck as I pull open
the door to the stairs what's bothering
him and he looks at me, his eyes
rock-steady on mine while his
head completes an orbit around his
nose, just looks carefully without saying a word.

Something's bothering
Food Truck today
but I don't know what and
we walk downstairs, he holds
on the rail with one hand and my
arm with the other, taking
each step one at a time, careful
now because years
ago he slipped on the
long icy steps out in

front of the building at Langdon and
fell and broke his hip. He says
Don't touch the
man's glasses and he says
go to the new house
and he says
ride in Bill's
truck and he
says *go home with Jack*
and something's
bothering him something's
bothering him but I
don't know
what because
he can't say and I can't hear.

What is bothering him
I don't know
and we walk down the hall
and we turn into my office
and he goes to the corner
and he knocks over the rubber plant
and soil spills over the carpet
and he sits down on the floor
and he pulls off his shoes
and he's yelling now
don't take off your clothes
don't take off your clothes
and he pulls off his socks
and he starts to pull down his pants
and he's yelling louder
party hat
party hat
which used to make the workers at Langdon come running

and he gets ready
to make
the best party hat he's ever made.

I look at him on the floor, sitting in the dirt
and say in a voice
as calm
and sure
and careful as I can make it
it's OK Barry
it's OK
you don't have to do that
we understand.

Food Truck looks up
he says quietly
in a voice falling apart
tumbling in on itself
Grandma's not feeling good
huge old man tears
flow out from his eyes
drip down his cheek
to make a small wet mark on his shirt.
All I can think to do
all I can ever do

is
rub
the back
of his
neck.

Chapter 3: MAN.i.f.e.s.t.o.: Disrupting Taxonomies of D{evil}op{MENTAL} Dis{ability}

"Naming is itself a form of power" (Valentine, 1998, 3.1)

1.
People labeled as having DEVELOPMENTAL DISABILITIES –
people now starting to reclaim their identity
by calling themselves **s e l f – a d v o c a t e s** –
have long been placed at the

                                                    borders

of cultural landscapes
by the social cartographers
of preposterously monosemic positivist science
employed by **eugenicist** special (so-called) education and human (so-called) services (Smith,
1999a; 2000).
Special educators,
like other human service and education professionals,
manipulate colonizing technologies
to mark the boundaries of perceived mind and body difference (Ryen & Silverman, 2000).
Inhabiting the *scaled marginalia*
of normalized and regulated cultural GHETTOS,
self-advocates have survived centuries of oppression and genocide
by a   *commodified*
                                 professionalized
                                 BEHAVIORIST
                                 death-making
                                 disability **service** industry
in support of a culture that creates and enhances difference through words (Kliewer and
Drake, 1998; Smith, 1999b; Trent, 1994).
                    Where would an alternative

to culturally normative scientific
representations
of people labeled as having developmental
disabilities
be located?
Would it be EMANCIPATORY?
What would be the scales of its song?
In what territories,
across what borders,
would it be heard?

*To begin answering these questions, I
have employed tools from visual (here, in
a published format) and sound (in a
presentation of another version of this
work [Smith, 2000]) poetry, often called
concrete poetry.*

*Like other explorers before me, I have
come to see that one way to understand
the social landscapes around me is
through the writing act (Richardson,
1994). In so doing, I also understand
that, as one poet says, "words are
knowledge... words are power" (Ross,
2000, Paragraph 1).*

I employ these specifically and
intentionally concretist tools to accentuate
and emphasize the inherent textuality of
this inquiry. For it is clear to me that "...
old grammatical-syntactical structures are
no longer adequate to advanced processes
of thought and communication..." (Solt,
1968, Paragraph 4).

2.

"...Everything is written, including ourselves"
(Tomasula, 1997).
Out of the thick <u>paste</u> of words,
cultural taxonomists have created
discursive holotypes of human difference
by using social codes of medicalized nomenclature.
They have reified **genera** and **species**
of *saturated* difference
by naming and codifying them:

anencephaly
Prader-Wili syndrome
cerebral palsy
cri-du-chat syndrome
microcephaly

Down syndrome

moderate cognitive disability
and all the numbered Others of them.

By naming Others, the self is defined
and created (Valentine, 1998).
Normative value is assumed for
the self. The naming of Others—
people with developmental disabilities
—focuses "...on deviation from the
normal" (Valentine, 1998, 2.1).
Taxonomies of developmental
disability describe and create not
just difference, but what is normal.
And yet normality is assumed rather
than stated overtly (named).

"[Experts] develop complex categories and sub-
categories of the other... of combining the
objectivity of science with an evaluation of

**ourselves as paragons of normality, health and
progress. 'Objective' categorization thus
simultaneously denies the significance of the
expert in the identification process, and confirms
the superiority of the expert over that which is
classified away—and indeed authenticates the
identify of expert in and through classification"**
(Valentine, 1998, 3.2).
It is in this way
that the role and importance
of special education is created and supported.
By naming and categorizing others,
special educators create *themselves*,
and create value for *themselves*,
by taking away the value of *others*.

But
as zoologist Terry Erwin (2000) has said,
speaking of the work of biological taxonomists,
"Words by themselves can't prove the existence of anything" (47).
This is an idea understood by those inhabiting the margins,
and not those who have created the center
by pushing others to the boundary.

Linton (1998) has pointed towards "**...the
vast realm of meaning-making that occurs
in metaphoric and symbolic uses of
disability**" (125) and that "**these devices
need to be analyzed in an array of cultural
products to understand their meanings
and functions, and to subvert their power.**"
(125). This is work that has clearly not begun
by the educational and human services
factory bosses of Western culture.

Linton goes on to discuss ways in which "**... figures of speech further objectify and alienate people with disabilities and perpetuate inaccurate information about disabled people's experience**" (p. 128).

The use of words
by dominating   human service
                                           and
                                           educational professionals
to create human difference in the service of a globalized capitalism
is a cultural practice that must end.
!!!
McLaren and Leonardo (1998)
have pointed out that the body is "...an ideological effect of language" (136).
Bodily and neurological differences are
created through linguistic nuance,
and are expressive
of an ideological stance.

                              Positivist Western science, in the form of
                              capitalist medical and educational industries,
                              creates Others through *taxonomic hierarchies*
                              of difference called disability (Smith, 1999a).
McLaren and Leonardo (1998)
go on to note that
"... the body houses various social
grammars and norms...
as discursive sites that are struggles over meaning" (136).
These struggles must include at the very least,
even if it has not yet been widely acknowledged,
the conflict between the binary
of a hegemonic capitalist exploitation and
a revolutionary critical theory as yet unspoken
by the preponderance of special(ized) education.

Yum.
Sound poet Henri Chopin (1967) points out ways in which words deny power
to those inhabiting cultural marginalia:

"It is impossible, one cannot continue
with the allpowerful Word, the Word
that reigns over all. One cannot
continue to admit it to every house,
and listen to it everywhere describe us
and describe events, tell us how to
vote, and whom we should obey... The
Word has created profit, it has
justified work, it has made obligatory
the confusion of occupation (to be
doing something), it has permitted life
to lie... it creates the inaccurate
SIGNIFICATION, which signifies
differently for each of us unless one
accepts and obeys... in what way can it
be useful to us? I answer: in no way"
(Chopin, 1967, Paragraph 1-3).

3.
The classroom,
says McLaren and Leonardo (1998)
is "the prison-house of knowledge,
a site of the totalization of regulative functions" (133).
This may be especially so
for the **dominating** behaviorist approach
that resides within the landscape of special education (Smith, 1999a).
Special education implies non-special educational,
practices that reside in the land of the normal.
The LANDSCAPE OF NORMALITY
is created from the culturally-geographic, pseudo-scientific features

of racism and eugenicism,
which place white, northern European culture at the center,
and self-advocates in a social taxonomy that is
"subhuman, an unnatural monstrosity" (Jenkins, 1993, 19).
The modernist eugenics movement,
which has allowed for the sterilization and assassination
of hundreds of thousands of people with disabilities
throughout the twentieth century around the globe,
supports essentialized rationalizations for difference (Allen, 1996; Kevles, 1999; Reilly and
Wertz, 1999).

4.
Stories told by people
who call themselves self-advocates
(people described by self-serving educational professionals
as having developmental disabilities) –
along with the stories told by family members,
sisters and brothers, mothers and fathers,
aunts uncles nieces nephews—
and stories told by educational assistants,
school administrators
special education coordinators
case managers
and all the other blah de blahs of bureaucratic educational and human services
    mumble-speak—
these stories
can no longer be sung in

NORMALIZING
frame-locked
bullshit
academic
language.

The language of standardizing academia
reinforces the razor-wired borders of marginalia.

Understanding words about developmental disability
as rising out of the primordial muck of
culturally-created metaphors
gives us opportunities for figuring out   who creates disability
                                                   where it is created
                                                   who is supported by it
                                                   how to denounce it.

Jargonate
(a word that precisely means itself, I think)
words are used to create territorialization
of knowledge about disability.
This language protects privileged understandings
residing in the landscapes of rehabilitation
from infection by viral outbreaks of
radical
critical
anti-normalized thought.

5.
The notion that writing can essentially duplicate so-called reality is so ~~STUPID~~.
Truth and Knowledge are dead and turning moldy.
Progress is a myth
perpetrated by the uniformed knowledge guards
of modernist science and disability research (Sale, 2000; Danforth, 1997).
Science is an ideology (Young, 1995).
Objectivity is a tool of oppression used by professional disability researchers.
The **T R A G I C** foundations of positivist disability epistemology
are afloat on a tectonic magma of postmodern critique.
It is *c r i t i c a l*, then, that words no longer be Hoovered out of the mouths of
                    self-advocates,
                    family members,
                    and their allies
by the suction-power of knowledge-simplifying

already-posthumous positivist academics.

All of this troubles the place of truth in (special) educational research,

the ^{TREMBLING} border between horrified fiction and *statuesque* non-fiction.

The line between them

in special education research representation

is the *hog* of chaos,

refusing to be held.

The stories told in/by/through critical post-modern ethnographers

will be frankly and overtly

fictional.

New postmodern

songs and stories and poems

will assert the complex and chaotic,

accentuate the processual, the synergistic,

the multiple, the experiential.

They will give value to the lands and peoples living at the margins of special (so-called)

education

research.

6.

New forms of educational research representation

must be created,

ones that will trouble

the cultural construction and reification of developmental disability,

of understanding how Western patriarchal society

inscribes disability on the bodies and lives of OTHERS.

Inquiry into the lives of self-advocates takes on (at least) two tasks:

explicating cultural metaphors,

and creating new ones.

Creating new metaphors

of what some call developmental disability

deconstructs old ones,

unpacking their social carpet-bags for a new journey.

This is a kind of research (re)presentation,
telling a story that is pissed-off and not afraid to admit it,
that needs to be authorized and privileged as authentic, legitimate
educational research.

7.
              Words

                                        are

      viruses.
In fact,
words infect us with culture.
Current educational taxonomies
of developmental disability
create difference
and reinforce the hegemony
of the Norm, of
REGULAR EDUCATION.
New forms of viral and contagious
research (re)presentations of the lives of self-advocates and their allies
must be created
THAT WILL UNDERMINE AND SUBVERT
these normalizing hierarchies.
They will be need to be **infectious cultural pathogens**
that corrupt and contaminate people's thinking, acting, and understanding
about what they insist on calling developmental disability.
For self-advocates have been clear:

> *"People must have a right to be recognized as the person they are, therefore they must not be labeled. Labels devalue us and must not be used to identify us"* (International League of Societies for Persons with Mental Handicap Committee on Self-Advocacy, 1996, p. 13).

◆ ◆ ◆

Referential Artifacts

Allen, G. (1996). Science misapplied: The eugenics age revisited. *Technology Review, 99* (August/September), 22-31.

Danforth, S. (1997). On what basis hope? Modern progress and postmodern possibilities. *Mental Retardation, 35,* 93-106.

Erwin, T. (2000). Typecast: The codes of nomenclature. *Whole Earth Review, 102,* 42.

International League of Societies for Persons with Mental Handicap Committee on Self-Advocacy (1996). *The beliefs, values and principles of self-advocacy.* Cambridge, MA: Brookline Books.

Jenkins, R. (1993). Incompetence and learning difficulties: Anthropological perspectives. *Anthropology Today, 9*(3), 16-20.

Kevles, D. (1999). Eugenics and human rights. *British Medical Journal, 319,* 435-8.

Kliewer, C. & Drake, S. (1998). Disability, eugenics and the current ideology of segregation: A modern moral tale. *Disability & Society, 13,* 95-111.

Linton, S. (1998). *Claiming disability: Knowledge and identity.* New York: New York University Press.

McLaren, P. & Leonardo, Z. (1998). Deconstructing surveillance pedagogy: *Dead Poet's Society. Studies in the Literary Imagination. 31*(1), 127-147.

Reilly, P. & Wertz, D. (1999). Eugenics: 1883-1970. *GeneLetter* (February 1, 1999).

Ross, E. (2000). Words. Retrieved from http://www.geocities.com/Athens/Agora/9095/words.html

Ryen, A. & Silverman, D. (2000). Marking boundaries: Culture as category work. *Qualitative Inquiry, 6,* 107-128.

Sale, K. (2000). Five facets of a myth. Retrieved from http://www.oneworld.org/analysis/articles/kirkpatricksale.html

Smith, P. (1999a). Drawing new maps: A radical cartography of developmental disabilities. *Review of Educational Research, 69*(2), 117-144.

Smith, P. (1999b). "I know how to do": Choice, control, and power in the lives of people with developmental disabilities. *Dissertation Abstracts International, 60*(11) A, 3965 (University Microfilms No. 9951862).

Smith, P. (2000). MAN.i.f.e.s.t.o.: A Poetics of D(EVIL)op[MENTAL] Dis{ABILITY}.
    Paper presented at Desegregating Disability Studies: An Interdisciplinary Conference,
    Syracuse, NY.

Smith, P. (2001). Inquiry cantos: A poetics of developmental disability. *Mental Retardation,*
    39, 379-390.

Solt, M. (1968). Concrete Poetry: A World View – Introduction. Retrieved from
    http://www.ubu.
    com/papers/solt/intro.html (Originally published by Indiana University Press).

Tomasula, S. (1997). Ways of seeing/Ways of being. *Electronic Book Review, 7* (Winter 1997-
    1998). Retrieved from http://www.altx.com/ebr/ebr6/6tomasula/6toma.htm

Trent, J. (1994). *Inventing the feeble mind: A history of mental retardation in the United*
    States. Berkeley: University of California Press.

Valentine, J. (1998). Naming the other: Power, politeness, and the inflation of euphemisms.
    Sociological Research Online, 3(4). Retrieved from http://www.socresonline.org.uk/
    3/4/7.html

Young, R. (1995). A place for critique in the mass media. Retrieved from
    http://www.human-nature.com/science-as-culture/paper15h.html

Chapter 4: whud i yam

I yam
mad
crazy
unbalanced
insane
psycho
lunatic
nuts
demented
mentally ill
batty
screwy
deranged
certifiable
gone around the bend
dotty
fallen off the deep end
moonstruck
bee headed
fruit loop
daft
gaga
climbed the stick
bonkers
halfbaked
kooky
left
blown your chips
disturbed
loony
cracked up

far gone
berserk
postal
lost his marbles
barking
mad as a hatter
wild
raving
corybantic
haywire
not all there
on a bender
crackbrained
loco
possessed
mentalist
buggy
dithyrambic
yampy
5150
of unsound mind
bats in his belfry
pulled a Cervantes
camel job
maniac
radge
barmy
bedlamite
screwball
brainsick
screw loose
section 8
cracked
sick

loopy
softheaded
high flier
balmy
whacko
squirrel bait
bats
tapped
off his chump
totally hat stand
psychjob
touched
crackers
unhinged
loon
bug hunting
unstable
crank
wackbasket
looney tunes
foogie
whacked
run amuck
mental
fruity
batshit

❖   ❖   ❖

Chapter 5: Split------ting the ROCK of {speci [ES]al} e.ducat.ion: FLOWers of lang[ue]age in >DIS<ability studIES

"...the flowers of rhetoric have real power to change reality, to penetrate it through and through, to 'split rocks'". (Franke, 2000, p. 143)

i. into int(r)o[ducat]ion scion science

this is

dis is

this is a test

this is a text

     about being a text

     about being a test

     about this is

     dis is

     dis is ab[il]ity

           [ill] city   a po-em

                   a po-me

                   a pomme filled word   tree

                                      dee

de   scribe ing

in   scribe ing

     b(in)g

     (b)e(ing)

     bing   cherries ways   in w{h}I{t}   ch

                                                  ch

   WARN   ING   ch

   WARN   ING   ch

   [will robinson]:   this new   th(ing)

   "the fallacy of ideational   this new disability studies   {thin}g

   mimesis is that it treats   this new   thin{g}

   ideas like objects that can

   be 'caught and held'..."   thinKING

   (Bernstein, 1987, p. 137)

```
                         new                    study(ing
                              disability    thing
              this new           b(rave)        thing
                    no                          thing:
```

```
                    what is it
                    what it is
                    how  it is
                    what it can tell      (talk to me now)
```

e	**DUCAT**	ion		educators
e	money coinage filthy euchre	ion	and	education
		scion	and	educatees
		science		tease

teasing out the meaning of

language re[present]ation

of   another narrative

another text

another WORD G{u}arden

(FLOWers)

(WOLF)

(talk to me now)

I am a person with a (hidden, elliptical) disability. I

hide it well

under my   hide

under my   skirts

of this otherwise **NORMATE** (bawdy) body.

My life and

existence is

l   abeled because of that

<in> some (con)texts with<in> the world I live <in> the

dis   abled

                                                             m

                                                             a

                                                             r

                                                             g

           off the narrated page   **<in>**

           of cultural texts.   **a**

                                                                    l

                                                                      i

                                                                      a

So, too, does my daughter.

But for her

        her body is   marked

                    mark[et]ed

by self-imposed   wounds

                    gaping holes

                    tiger stripes   to   get the red   out

                                      get the pain   out

                                      get the lead   out

                                    get the world <in>

                                       the word <in>

reflecting her difference

on the mirror of her body

stigmata

{stigma}   ta

              ta ta

              bye-bye

              gotta go to the--edge here

              made by   this   edge here

                              this   razor ear

                                  cut it off

                                  cut it out   about

                                  (the) scream

this is a text about being a text about describing ways in which about new disability studies thinking about can tease out about the language and representation about disability in education about what it is about how it is about you would have been instructed where about

                                                                    to turn
                                                                    to turn
                                                                    to turn

talk to me now.

                                    ◆   ◆   ◆

ii. notes on form. {but not ulaic} to be read in an order that is not pre(pro)scribed.

"Style and form are as ideological as content and interpretation" (Bernstein, 1987, p. 127). This is a kind of rule. The form is ideological so it must be opened up. This is a writing about writing. This writing is about writing and it is a form. We call it a form. Should we say something now about form? So I will. Is there an echo? Hello? Is someone there? Talk.

Like a can. Of worms. This is a disabilities studies text a new kind of a text.

I have used this form before. In writing on the page I did it (Smith, 2001a) and in another writing on a page I did it (Smith, 2001b) but only a little. Talk to me now. Now? The talking we do is through words and we write them down. Write them down on the page. This page. Perhaps we should say something now about form. So I will. Is there an echo? Hello? Is someone there? To me.

And in speaking I did it (Smith, 2000). I will talk about it here. About doing it. Here is where I will talk about it and I will.

We know one thing. Words do not mean things but they mean other words only other words and that is all. Other words and sentences sometimes. We have known it and I have said it before. We have said it before and it is a very good saying of it, to others, to be read by them, in words. It would be good to say something about form. So I will. Is there an echo? Hello? Is someone there? Now.

Others have said it before as I have said too (Smith, 1999a). This thing has a word it is incommensurability. And the word means that words do not mean things but only other words and sentences sometimes.

All of the words that we say and we say them very much are another thing which is that they are all ideological. This is another thing that I have said before too (Smith, 1999a; Smith, 1999b). And I said it before in another way too (Smith, 2004).

Talk to me now.

Talk to me now.

Talk to me now.

Words change what we look at and describe, becoming the language itself, becoming the meaning we give it.

This way of putting words together "...draws attention both to the non-representational capacities of language as material, and to the political power inherent in new writing... by reinventing syntax, opposing and questioning grammar... we open language and thereby society to new organizational alternatives... [It can be] transgressive: it succeeds in dismantling and rewiring the social and corporal body..." (Doris, 2001, Paragraph 2-3).

And here is a thing that another man said, before the thing that the two men said, he said: "Language is the first technology, the extension of the body outward toward an articulation, a *forging*, of the world, which is immediately transformed by this act, hence a *forgery*" Bernstein, 1987, p. 125).

"...we can think of the body as an ideological effect of language" (McLaren & Leonardo, 1998, p. 136).

Whatever we say changes what we say about the thing we say: "that basic truth became the Heisenberg uncertainty principle: that whatever you studied you also changed" (Crichton, 1995, p. 249).

Now here is a thing that should be said and so I will say it. In special education we number bodies (Stone, 1997) and that is an ideological effect of language. Words are always ideological (Davis, 2002). Bodies and minds that have disabilities are ideological and we make them ideological by our words. This language is a making of the world as we see it.

To make "...the modern nation-state not simply language but bodies and bodily practices also had to be standardized, homogenized, and normalized" (Davis, 2002, p. 106). And what is lost in this word practice, in this world practice, "...is the irregular, the nonquantifiable, the nonstandard or nonstandardizable, the erratic..." (Bernstein, 1993, p. 605), which is exactly and precisely what we call disability.

I will make words in a new way so that the new words will not number bodies. This way of making words will be a way of making words that talks about words and their making and what the making of them makes.

This writing that I am doing here is a writing about writing kind of doing. It is a writing about writing kind of doing which is a good kind of writing doing. It is a kind of writing doing that changes the kind of writing doing that some writers do. Other writers do not. I think it is important to do the kind of writing doing that I have been writing about doing, in order to show and to see what that kind of writing doing might be doing. This kind of writing doing is a kind of doing, it is not a done thing, it is a doing. So it is a kind of writing doing that you do, but it is not a kind of writing doing that is a done thing. It is only doing, only just doing, never done.

Words "...construct the objects which then come to populate our world" (Madill, Jordon, & Shirley, 2000, p. 12.) The words of special education make the bodies that are numbered they make them and if the making of them is a thing which is not good then we need to change the way the words are which would be a good thing and so I will do it here.

A man and a woman said this and it is a very important saying, that "language is constitutive of social practices" (Wilson & Lewiecki-Wilson, 2001, p. 3).

These words will "...tap into the power of etymology. Etymological insight... involves an understanding of the origins of the construction of social, cultural, psychological, political, economic, and educational artifacts and the ways they shape our subjectivities" (Kincheloe, 2001, p. 687).

Another thing to say about this way of writing is that it is parataxic. You should look it up in a dictionary it is a good word. I'll wait while you look it up. There you're back. It is a good word and a good thing.

This new way of writing must be it certainly must be it is required to be it simply has to be simply and irrevocably this: an "...ironic and blasphemous (re) writing of the disabled body in order to (re) invent alternative emancipatory subjectivities" (Erevelles, 2001, p. 93).

Talk to me now.

And it is ludic too this writing is which is a good thing and is another word that you should look up in a dictionary it is a good kind of word and I'll wait while you look it up. There you're back again so soon.

The awful thing that must be said is that "...nearly everything that's been written or said is wrong" (Crichton, 1995, p. 232).

This thing is a form that some will call Language Poetry and some will call Concrete Poetry and some will call it other things, but the important thing is that we can write about education and disability and special education in a new way so that we do not write about it in an old way, a way that another man has said and he called it a word he would like to "call it a *necroidiocracy*, ideas stiffened by rigor mortis wounding flesh with their rigidity and their techno-rationality..." (Bernstein, 1987, p. 124-125).

Talk to me now.

Talk to me now.

"Parataxis is crucial: the internal, autonomous meaning of a new sentence is heightened, questioned, and changed by the degree of separation or connection that the reader perceives with regard to the surrounding sentences" (Perelman, 1993, p. 313). And most of what they will mean will be a metaphor which is a thing that I will talk about later.

Talk to me now.

Talk to me now.

Talk to me now.

Talk to me now.

Talk to me now.

Talk to me now.

Finally, this writing is a bricolage, and so is disability studies, and what disability studies can bring to education is to "...study the workings of a particular discipline... such a disciplinary study would be conducted more like a Foucauldian genealogy where scholars would study the social construction of the discipline's knowledge bases, epistemologies, and knowledge production methodologies... In this genealogical context they would explore the discipline as a discursive system of regulatory power with its propensity to impound knowledge within arbitrary and exclusive boundaries" (Kincheloe, 2001, p. 683-684).

iii. pounding on a rock. (The Bobs, 1988)
pound on dis here
dis ability rock
and role
and roll
and control and control and control
dis rock abilly
hill   billy
ill   bil(ity)
dis rock please
dis please
dis ease
dis able tease
dis able tease stud
dis able tease stud ease
       can de(in)scribe w{rough}t IRON[-ic] metaphor (mat)

be   **it**   **re**   **us**
  cause   **can**   **mind** **of**

> "...the referentiality of acts of language to anything but other acts of language... [It] supposes that a hermeneutics of suspicion (resisting readers) and deconstruction (texts betraying their ostensible aims) will expose... [education's] complicity in supporting and advancing middle-class ideologies of power... a hermeneutics which exposes capitalist, colonialist, racist, and sexist ideologies will help democratize a world presently closed to many marginalized groups" (Gregory, 1998, p. 35-36).

he forgot to say ableist they always do
hoo ya
the   profundity
jocularity
homogeneity
irony   of meta-ph(l)or (mat)
      the irony of metal floor mats
      is dat (a)

"metaphors guide our thinking and seeing, and they pervade how we understand the world" (Hsusu, 2001, p. 175).

oh, and uhmm

"metaphors frame and structure meaning..." (Becker, 1994, p. 384)

which is ok, no think wrong or right, whether i'm wrong or right, whether i'm wrong nothing wrong ring rang rung wrong with metaphors in and of themselves (heck, Mell, I better not be sayin that there were, lawsa me no, bein a poet and all, metaphors er my stock and trade, as it were, dontcha know, so to speak) (easy) (heck, Mell, "it has become possible to view all language as being metaphorical..." (Franke, 2000, p. 138) is what I'm tryin to say here)

but (h)Our   thin (king)

not the queen but the king

down by the old....

is forced to ride in the slow lane uv

                textual
                processual
                sexual
                {tr}aff®ic **{A}**

required by the metaph(l)or (mat) police of so-called

common(bourgeois)-sense, trans[parent] texts (Lather, 1996). Count(1234)er

t(w)o this is (must) be **THE** work of dis able tease stud tease,

                "exerting some control over metaphorical representation in language, theory, politics, and artistic practice..." (Sandahl, 1999, p. 13),

(re)COGnizing {t}hat

                "metaphors are not innocuous artistic flourishes... but powerful discursive structures that can misrepresent, define, and confine people with disabilities" (Sandahl, 1999, p. 14).

all texts – all special texts – all species (of) all – all species awful offal

all special education texts hide behind

                trans [parent]
                common
                comMAN

                     sense

cents
$ and cents
lan(guage)
 gauging the size of it all
measuring it out
speci(es)al rulers and tools
ruling us, ruling (THEM)
disguising itself in a new   ALL HALLOWS EVE costume
ALL GALLOWS EVE

(heh, me and Freddie Kruger)

(never even saw the movie, just heard about it)

"...the literal itself must be apprehended as metaphorical in its basic constitution. This ironic predicament is, in fact, written into the very term literal, itself based on the metaphor of the written character, the letter, being used to stand for a certain kind of meaning. The letter is itself nothing but a figure, a concrete image, for this kind of literal meaning that is purportedly devoid of figurativeness. And when presumably unrhetorical, fact-stating discourse itself is shown to be never given without presupposing a prior process, an originating movement, of transfer of meaning that is, in the deepest sense, metaphorical, then metaphor has become universal in scope..." (Franke, 2000, p. 140).

it's **all** metaph(l)or (mat) then
the literal
the limitable
becoming, through poetic deconstruction
(tearing it down with a wordy rotten wrecking crane)
(talk to me now)
a process of semiotic unparceling

semiosis
halitosis

BECOMING
the liminal
the illuminatable

the illimitable

and in addition
    subtraction
    multiplication
    division

"Because words are part of language and language is a communal practice, there can be no use of language that transcends the sociability and biases of any linguistic community... they are therefore ideological by definition." (Davis, 2002, p. 120).

ideo-logical = idiot logic
words log[strawberry]

    jammed
    jellied
    jelly roll (rock and morton) into reified
                      commodified
                      latinate
      super**{MAN}** struc tures
                      struck   chores

filching the   homogenized
               homophobic
               enqueered
               enfreaked   bawdy
                                    badly
                                  bloody
                                  bodies and   mined
                       (moth)er {father} lode
                                minds
               of the counter-normate subaltern.
        (PHEW) SAY THAT 10 TIMES FAST

Instead, medicalized ventriloquizing "...discourses normalize modes of intelligibility and construct particular regimes of truth as legitimate" (McLaren, Leonardo, & Allen, 1999, p. 140).

In the w[h]or[le]d wor{l}d of e{ducat}ion

In the w[h]or[le]d wor{l}d of dis able tease
In the whored wired weird world
In the horrid word world of species all Ed ducat science ions

               "...it is the social meaning
               of words that have power"
               (Russell, 1998, p. 16).

it is in the   **LANGUE**

        tongue
        lingo
        patois
        jargon

Ford	Fido
Chryser	Rover
Chevy	Spot
Toyota	Buddy

        languishing mouth bodies
        the slung word (car)   (pet)
        that's where the power is, jack, know what I'm sayin'?

power jack
car jack
jack knife
what we need to do is to   knife through
                       knife through the water
                       swimming laps in the Olympic size pool of ableism
cut it all out!
Van Gogh's ear!
my daughter's skin!
Tom Dick and Harry!
The Hardy Boys! Nancy Drew! Frank Sinatra! (who?)
      knife through
      these disability transparent commonsense bourgeois liberal
metaphor   sets
knife   sets
deconstruct and explicate the socio-cultural metaphors of modernist Western
shoot 'em up   Clint Eastwood
                John Wayne
                Henry Fonda

                    Henry Ford
                                        disability.
(every time i go back to find something i have to stop and put something in
me and jack kerouac's crazy limber limbo dead body interrupting myself with these birdwalks
      hey hey

talk to me now)
see the thing of it is we **ALL**
every golldang un a us
                "...adopt or be adopted by perspectives which then guide and limit... [our] view
                of the social world... metaphors constitute rather than exemplify these
                perspectives. Metaphor is not so much a word or a sentence as a conceptual
                system or model" (Manning, 1991, p. 72).
and the   problemo
the   proBLEM{ISH}
with these metaph(l)ors these floor mats these florid images these forms these mor(ph)s
and I ain't sayin here that metaphors are all bad, shoot no
we can't help it
honest officer, i just couldn't help myself, i just had to steal that bus
no, see, the problem that we got here dontcha know
is that there is a
d**ANGER** will robinson crusoe swiss family
d**ANGER** in the "...mistaken conflation of words and identities...
                The risk is that metaphor may be transformed from an insightful
                resemblance into an all-embracing world view" (Manning, 1991, p. 72).
yessir, that's it right there, dagnabit.
OK.
So.
I'll let ol' Norm say it: "Humans are always already tangled
                                    up in a second-hand world of meanings, and have no direct
                                    access to reality. Reality as it is known is lodged in narrative
                                    texts which mediate the real" (Denzin, 1996, p. 526).
                                    Got that?
                                    Hey—you there—

                                        talk to me now.
        Well, ok, but then: "...discourses normalize modes of
                                intelligibility and construct particular regimes of truth as
                                legitimate" (McLaren, Leonardo, & Allen, 1999, p. 140).
Which, as we all know, "...denies subjects their right to name the world" (McLaren,
Leonardo, & Allen, 1999, p. 140).
Well that's it right there in a nutshell.   disability
                                                dishabille stud (ebaker)
                                                disability
                (I'm trying to get it out now, honest, its like some goddam burroughsian
                lip-surge it won't stop)
                                        stud tease
                                        a palpitative moose base
                                        disability studies—that's it!—
                                        DISA BILK—bilking them all
                                of   their words
                                                their worlds
                                                their whirled weird whored
                disability
                                        studies brings to this species of
                special
                education
it's all about the money, you know, the ducats—
                                        the opportunity for people with disabilities to take
                (no rant, thanks Utah)
                                        control of the metaphoric
                                        meta-flouric
                                        re-presentation
                                        done over again performance
                                        of their
                too much already mined
                                        minds and bodies, and in so doing,
                                        to take control of their world.
These metal floor mats, these   symphonic

sympathetic
symbols   of dishabille tease
"...are inescapably inflected and entrained by the flows and circuits of capital. Slingshot into a fluctuating universe of meaning, symbols and metaphors partake of a unique semiotics that is utterly dependent upon intersecting moments of time, space, and place. We are constituted by these symbols that we are given in order to 'perform' the narratives of our lives, often in contexts not of our choosing..." (McLaren, 1999, p. xxxix).

iv. Another little note on form(ation): looting the ludic
Patti Lather   wrote
rote
root (roto)   tiller
rotilla the hun
away goes trouble down the
a great little piece back pretty near a decade ago,
talking and ranting (thanks Utah) about her work and her   rigged
rattan
writing. Given (taken) what I've just   talked about
walk(ed) about
in terms of   metaphor
meta-fluoride
toothpaste
meta fluoric acid
about correspondence (strange letters sent from far away) theories of truth,
WHODUNIT   about language
GAUGING THE SIZE OF power, what she has to say makes a lot of (DOLLARS AND)
sense to me:

"To speak so as to be understood immediately is to speak through the production of the transparent signifier, that which maps easily onto taken-for-granted regimes of meaning. This runs a risk that endorses, legitimates, and reinforces the very structure of symbolic value that must be overthrown" (1996, p. 528).

Well, duh.

instead
bedstead
she argues for   "...other practices of representation that decenter
                                  traditional realistic narrative forms" (p. 527).
She calls for a way of   making texts
                                  taking mex

that   "makes space for returns, silence,
                                                  interruptions, self-criticism, and points to
                                                  its own incapacity. Such a practice ignites
                                                  in writing and reading what is beyond the
                                                  word and rationally accessible, gesturing
                                                  toward a textual practice that works at
                                                  multiple levels in sounding out an
                                                  audience with ears to hear" (p. 532).

She asserts (two mints in one) the importance of

                                                  "producing the unconscious as the work
                                                  of the text, working the ruins of a
                                                  confident social science as the very ground
                                                  from which new practices of ...
                                                  representation might take shape" (p. 539),
and the need   "...to construct risky practices of textual
                                                  innovation in order to perform the very
                                                  tensions that this essay has addresses: to
                                                  be of use in a time when the old stories
                                                  will not do" (p. 541).

My work as a bricoleur is to work these ruins—to take some of the textual practices I know
from so called L=A=N=G=U=A=G=E and Concrete poetic forms, understanding some of
the political and cultural under/overtones ensconced therein, and apply those tools fertile
crescent wrench
                                                  screwing the driver
                                                  hammer   (pounding on a)
to the growing body (literally) of work   lift that bale, tote that barge
        in a humanities approach to disability studies—and using the vehicle of disability
        studies, so constructed, as a way to explore education, special or otherwise.

In doing so, I hear some critical theorist's saying: but its all just word play, it's all

                 ludicity

(clearly **NOT**   lucidity, heh). And that a critical theory approach is incommensurable

   with that

(this) kind of ludicity.

To which I have

2

responses. First, as Ralph Waldo Emerson said,

                "A foolish

                consistency is

                the hobgoblin

                of little

                minds..."

My work, as any good bricoleur, is to

loot the ludic!

(thanks, Julia, for mishearing that word). By looting the ludic, I mean finding what is useful in ludicity that can be productively used in creating emancipatory rather than oppressive possibilities, and stealing it, using it for those ends.

This writing is   hypercatalectic

                      metonymic

                      paranomatic

                      anacoluthonic

                      palinodic

                      gruic

                      syzygic

                      periphrastic

                      pleonasmic

                      echoistic

                      paraliptic

                      aposiopetic

                      macaronic

                      elliptic

                      caesuraic

                      neologistic

epizeuxic
occupatiotic
asyndetonic

v. "...bodies of knowledge and knowledge of bodies." Lather, 1996, p. 541)
Species offal Ed ducat science
(special education)
is all rapped up in eu**(YOU)**genics, which we've known for a long time now (Kliewer &
    Drake, 1998).
It is a process   of body numbering,
                         of revulsion,
                         of disgust,
                         of regularity,
                         of the **CREATION**
                         of **DEVIATION**
(Davis, 1995; Sibley, 1995; Thomson, 1996; 1997).
Where'd it all come from? **INDUSTRIAL**   ization
                           MODERN   ization
                           MECHAN   ization
                           STANDARD   ization
                           PROFESSIONAL   ization
                           SECULAR   ization
                                        (Thomson, 1996, p. 11).
and its all tied together with {numb}ers, violating
                                    violenting
                                            numbing integers.
Just as the eu**(YOU)**genists did (and still do), special education creates

↓

                        species of difference—

a taxonomy
a tax on me

through testing processes that assign numeric values to human beings:
"In reducing learning to a test score,
policymakers seek to make the
knowledge of disparate individuals
commensurable...once knowledge is
reified in this way, it can be
manipulated and described in the
same fashion that one is accustomed
to manipulating and describing
products (commodities) of all
kinds... as complex human and
social processes are more and more
flattened into crude representations
that will conform to the logic of
commodity production and
exchange" (De Lissovoy & McLaren,
2003, p. 133).
Yeah, it's all about "...a quantification of the human body..." (Davis, 1995, p. 11-12), a
construct of "political arithmetic" (Porter, 1986, in Davis, 1995, p. 26).
                    ...a quantification of the human mind...
                    ...a quantification of the human soul...

Knowledge becomes a commodity, a   thing to be
                                    bought and sold
                                    and bodies

(especially bodies of those who are   women
                                       working class
                                       people of color
                                       queer)

are   made different
       differentiated

ENQUEERED

through the work of special educators:

"Schooling... is... a site of surveillance
and the marking and reproduction of
power, where working class bodies are
located as inferior, quarantined
within designated spaces of formal
identity, dissected by the white gaze
of power, masticated by the jaws of
capital, made receptive to the
command metaphors of formal
citizenship, and transformed into
semiotic battlegrounds..." (McLaren,
1999, p. xxxiii).

Some fun, huh?

Put plainly, "...the concept of disability is a function of a concept of normalcy" (Davis, 1995,
p. 2). That which is   not   normal
                                                        must be ab   normal
                                                        must be   other.

And

"...the cultural other and the cultural
self operate together as opposing twin
figures that legitimate a system of
social, economic, and political
empowerment justified by
physiological differences... Normate,
then, is the constructed identity of
those who, by way of the bodily
configurations and cultural capital
they assume, can step into a position of
authority and wield the power it
grants them" (Thomson, 1997, p. 8).

All of this happens through a
    process of forgetting:

"What is not worth remembering is
often constructed as 'normal'"
(Norquay, 1999, p. 3).

Forgetting's a funny thing: it   "...produces a form of ignorance... forgetting is the effect of
                                   an active process... forgettings work to make the boundaries
                                   and demarcations of the dominant culture invisible..."
                                   (Norquay, 1999, p. 1-2).

The question for disability studies is,

"who does 'normal' serve?"

(Russell, 1998, p. 19).

it ain't me babe, no no no

it ain't the deviations, the   (h)extremes   (Davis, 1995)
                                     Supremes
                                     phonemes
                                     bulimes

Davis, he say "...THE VERY TERM THAT
PERMEATES OUR CONTEMPORARY
LIFE – THE NORMAL – IS A
CONFIGURATION THAT ARISES IN A
PARTICULAR MOMENT. IT IS A PART
OF A NOTION OF PROGRESS, OF
INDUSTRIALIZATION, AND OF
IDEOLOGICAL CONSOLIDATION OF
THE POWER OF THE BOURGEOISE"
(1995, p. 49).

And the (so-called, only temporarily and forgotten) able-bodied, looking
(because "disability is a specular moment" (Davis, 1995, p. 12))
at the (so-called, permanently and always re-membered) dis-abled freak, sees

        "...a hypervisible text against which the viewer's indistinguishable body fades
        into a seemingly neutral, tractable, and invulnerable instrument of the
        autonomous will, suitable to the uniform abstract citizenry democracy
        institutes"
        (Thomson, 1996, p. 11).

It's hypervisible, oh yeah

                that text
                those bodies
                these minds.

"The act of seeing is a de facto act of violence" (McLaren, Leonardo, & Allen, 1999, p. 143).

a dismembering	violence
a dis(re)membering	violence
a forgetting	violence
a forgotten	violence vio(la)(ess)ence

dis-membering as an act of {re}moving member-ship (mother-ship) from a community of those who would otherwise be, but never quite are, peers.

You getting' a FEEL for   who normal serves?
the maid and butler
waiting on them
subservient
SUB servant

      You getting' a FEEL for   the fact that I am, with others,
"...deeply disillusioned with Western liberal political philosophy and processes, deeming liberalism to have corrupted itself in the pursuit of a status quo favoring middle-class power groups. Liberalism has, furthermore, constructed an array of ideologies to disguise social oppression and to preserve the status quo..." (Gregory, 1998, p. 35).

What we haven't figgered out is that   DISABILITY is the rule
                                                 the norm
                                                 the mean
                                                 the median
                                               the average
                                               the common

All of us will spend time during our lives living with what we call disability: "...difference is what all of us have in common" (Davis, 2002, p. 26).

We of the bourgeoisie (we have met the enemy and they is us)—

we have been	captivated
	arrested
	enthralled
	grabbed
	enamored
	bewitched
	enslaved

seized
ensnared

by this **STOOPID** Western
modernist positivist ventriloquizing
masquerading disguising enfleshing
"...scientific view, which depends upon the fantasy
of objectivity and sees regularity rather than
exceptionality as founding epistemology..."
(Thomson, 1996, p. 3).

Who does normal serve?　　SPECIal education.
　　　　　　　　　　　　SPECIal educators.
Individual and SPECIfic SPECial educators
(we can't get off the hook)
as cultural representatives of liberalist ideology, unintentionally
(sorry dear, i forgot)
"...develop complex categories and
subcategories of the other, which
carry the wonderful modernist
hope... of combining the
objectivity of science with an
evaluation of ourselves as paragons
of normality, health and progress.
Objective categorization thus
simultaneously confirms the
superiority of the expert over that
which is classified away—and
indeed authenticates the identity
of expert in and through
classification" (Valentine, 1998,
3.2).

vi. what to do.
1. We need new tongues—new langues of dis-ability, new speakings about normal, new kinds
of texts that can REpresent "...thinking the multiple (im)possibilities for thought outside

taken-for-granted structures of intelligibility" (Lather, 1996, p. 540). This text I am writing here is not the right best example,   only
                                                                                                    merely

one among many possibilities:

a new word (dis)order.

2. In addition to new ways of rePRESENTNG, we need a different kind of ideology (we won't escape that it will be ideological): "Disability studies demands a shift from the ideology of normalcy, from the rule and hegemony of normates, to a vision of the body [and mind] as changeable, unperfectable, unruly, and untidy" (Davis, 2002, p. 39). This kind of thinking will be

        a thinking of difference
        a thinking of freaks
        a thinking of   impermanence
                           margination
                           promiscuity
                           unkemptedness
                           disorder
                           anomalousness
                           exceptionality
                           peculiarity
                           unaccustomable

3. We will need a new kind of research   (in education)
                                                          (in special education)
                                                          (in social sciences)
that allows for and encourages a kind of inquiry that arises from DISCiplines
                                                                      DISCourses
outside of those we're used to seeing in those lands:

        research that is irregular
        research that is nonlinear
        research that is artistic
        research that is irrational

This kind of research will be counter to typical academic exploration, where "...thought tends to be rationalized—subject to examination, paraphrase, repetition, mechanization, reduction. It is treated: contained and stabilized" (Bernstein, 1993, p. 605).

It will be counter to that; it will be   destabilizing

                                                 uncontained

                                                 untreated

Such a research will not explore traditional avenues—instead, it will look down little alleys, hidden side streets, dirty passageways, those spaces filled with crumpled newspaper, discarded boxes, bits of crumpled metal, a torn magazine cover—places overlooked and looked over and ignored by normate inquiry. It will be a research that acknowledges that the humanities and the arts has much to offer, both in form and function.

It will be a virulent research.

It will be a pissed off research (thanks, Linda).

4. And it all will be done—these researches, these languages, these ideologies—by those whose voices and signs and silences and lives have not been heard or seen or attended to by the normative educational institutions in our culture—institutions that destroy the lives of people with disabilities, but the lives of all of us.

◆   ◆   ◆

Referenciated Artifactoids

Becker, G. (1994). Metaphors in disrupted lives: Infertility and cultural constructions of continuity. *Medical Anthropological Quarterly, 8,* 383-410.

Bernstein, C. (1987). Living tissue/Dead ideas. *Social Text, 16,* 124-135.

Bernstein, C. (1993). What's art got to do with it? The status of the subject of the humanities in the age of cultural studies. *American Literary History, 5,* (597-615).

Bobs, The (1988). *Songs for tomorrow morning.* (CD). Kaleidoscope Records.

Crichton, M. (1995). *The lost world.* New York: Alfred A. Knopf.

Davis, L. (1995). *Enforcing normalcy: Disability, deafness, and the body.* New York: Verso.

Davis, L. (2002). *Bending over backwards: Disability, dismodernism and other difficult positions.* New York: New York University Press.

De Lissovoy, N. & McLaren, P. (2003). Educational 'accountability' and the violence of capital: A Marxian reading. *Journal of Education Policy, 18* (2), 131-143.

Doris, S. (2001). After language poetry. *OEI, 7-8.*

Erevelles, N. (2001). In search of the disabled subject. In J. Wilson & C. Lewieki-Wilson (Eds.) *Embodied rhetorics: Disability in language and culture* (pp. 92-111). Carbondale, IL: Southern Illinois University Press.

Franke, W. (2000). Metaphor and the making of sense: The contemporary metaphor renaissance. *Philosophy and Rhetoric, 33,* 137-153.

Godfrey, N. & Smith, P. (June 2002). A Raucous, Hybrid Blues: Creating An Un/nerving Un/holy Entangled Alliance Between Whiteness Studies and Disability Studies. Second Annual Second City Conference on Disability Studies and Education, Chicago, IL.

Gregory, M. (1998). Fictions, facts, and the fact(s) of(in) fictions. *Modern Language Studies, 28.3, 4,* 3-40.

Hsusu, L. (2001). On metaphors on the position of women in academia and science. *NORA, 9*(3), 172-181.

Kincheloe, J. (2001). Describing the bricolage: Conceptualizing a new rigor in qualitative research. *Qualitative Inquiry, 7,* 679-692.

Kliewer, C. & Drake, S. (1998). Disability, eugenics and the current ideology of segregation: A modern moral tale. *Disability & Society, 13,* 95-111.

Madill, A., Jordan, A., & Shirley, C. (2000). Objectivity and reliability in qualitative analysis: Realist, contextualist, and radical constructionist epistemologies. *British Journal of Psychology, 91,* 1-20.

Manning, P. (1991). Drama as life: The significance of Goffman's changing use of the theatrical metaphor. *Sociological Theory, 9,* 70-86.

McLaren, P. (1999). *Schooling as a ritual performance: Toward a political economy of educational symbols and gestures* (3rd ed.). NY: Rowman & Littlefield Publishers, Inc.

McLaren, P. & Leonardo, Z. (1998). Deconstructing surveillance pedagogy: *Dead Poet's Society. Studies in the Literary Imagination, 31*(1), 127-147.

McLaren, P., Leonardo, Z., & Allen, R. (1999). The gift of si(gh)ted violence: Toward a discursive intervention into the organization of capitalism. *Discourse, 21.2,* p. 139-162.

Norquay, N. (1999). Identity and forgetting. *The Oral History Review, 26*(1), 1-12.

Perelman, B. (1993). Parataxis and narrative: The new sentence in theory and practice. *American Literature, 65,* 313-324.

Porter, T. (1986). *The rise of statistical thinking 1820-1900.* Princeton, NJ: Princeton University Press.

Russell, M. (1998). *Beyond ramps: Disability at the end of the social contract.* Monroe, ME: Common Courage Press.

Sibley, David (1995). *Geographies of exclusion: Society and difference in the west.* New York: Routledge.

Smith, P. (1999). Ideology, politics, and science in understanding developmental disabilities. *Mental Retardation, 37,* 71-72.

Smith, P. (1999). Drawing new maps: A radical cartography of developmental disabilities. *Review of Educational Research, 69* (2), 117-144.

Smith, P. (Oct. 2000). MAN.i.f.e.s.t.o.: A Poetics of D(EVIL)op[MENTAL] Dis{ABILITY}. Desegregating Disability Studies: An Interdisciplinary Conference, Syracuse, NY.

Smith, P. (2001b). Inquiry cantos: A poetics of developmental disability. *Mental Retardation, 39,* 379-390.

Smith, P. (2001a). MAN.i.f.e.s.t.o.: Disrupting Taxonomies of D{evil}op{MENTAL} Dis{ability}. *Taboo: The Journal of Education and Culture, 5* (1), 27-36.

Smith, P. (2004). Whiteness, normal theory, and disability studies. *Disability Studies Quarterly, 24* (2).

Stone, D. (1997). *Policy paradox: The art of political decision making.* New York: W. W. Norton and Company.

Thomson, R. G. (1996). Introduction: From wonder to error – A genealogy of freak discourse in modernity. In R.G. Thomson (Ed.) *Freakery: Cultural spectacles of the extraordinary body* (pp. 1-19). New York: New York University Press.

Thomson, R. G. (1997). *Extraordinary bodies: Figuring physical disability in American culture and literature.* New York: Columbia University Press.

Valentine, J. (1998). Naming the other: Power, politeness and the inflation of euphemisms. *Sociological Research Online, 3*(4), n.p.

Chapter 6: an ILL/ELLip(op)tical *po* – ETIC/EMIC/Lemic/litic *po*st® uv ed DUCAT ion *re*cherché *re*pres©entation

"There is nothing outside the text." (Derrida, 1976, pp. 226-27)

How I got here: In the late 1990's, I began work exploring the role of choice, control, and power in the lives of people with developmental disabilities, their families, and the people who support them (Smith, 2000). I was fortunate to be mentored by Corrine Glesne, an absolutely wonderful ethnographer (1989; 1998; 2003; Busier, Clark, Esch, Glesne, Pigeon, & Tarule, 1997; Martin & Glesne, 2002). Corrine taught me much about the qualitative research tradition, both in and out of the broad field of education (Glesne, 2006).

Corrine explored ways in which her research could be represented in non-traditional forms. As a poet, she became interested in ways in which poetry could be used as a representational mode for her research, developing a style that she called poetic transcription (Glesne, 1997; 2004). Informed by her work and thinking, I adopted a poetic transcription style in some of my own writing (Smith, 2000; 2001a; 2004). Later, I extended and transcended this poetic in other work, borrowing from approaches used by conceptual, postmodernist, and other post-poets (Smith, 1999a; 2000; 2001b; in press; Smith & Godfrey, 2002).

Here, I will outline what I would call a poetics of representation, arising out of what others have referred to as a dismodernist perspective (Davis, 2002). This poetics is almost literally a moving target—it changes as fast as I write it down, for the act of writing it influences the poetic (which influences the writing, which influences the poetic: it is, literally, a writhing writing). This writing about research is seeking to become, as Lather says, "the other/outside of the logic of noncontradiction" (2003, p. 4).

The way I see it (today, sitting at this particular desk, overlooking the waters of Lake Superior, in the throes of a tremendous gale not unlike the way the words are coming to me here),

this wri(GH)t[H]ing is   wrought
                           hand-carved

hacked out of

what Weathers (1980) calls Grammar B:

"the quasi-amorphousness of a memo, the ongoing chain effect of thought association, the incorporation of notes directly into a text" (p. 10).

This   writing

this   wry thing

this   writhing

    is   tangential

    is   tan genital

    is   tan gentian

        is   repetitive

        is   repetitive

        is   repetitive

        is   repetitive

            is   word-heavy

            is   word-**HEAVY**

            is   whored-heaven

It is a PO – etic/emic/lemic/litic of research.

It is not   whole

        (w)hole

        It is a hole, a howl, a haul (away me maties):

        KNOWLEDGE CAN ONLY EVER BE PARTIAL.

        And

        "all readings are misreadings" (Lather, 2003, p.1).

        by definition.

        Here, I'm a   **kleptomaniac** of stories

            bricklayer of stories

            grocer of stor(i)es

            lepidopterist of stories

      expl   oring

      expl   aining

expl   icating

the moths of narrative (and, so, research).
They are   moths

mouths

mouthings
funny word slurps/slaps/slops.
Inside the cocoons of the words scattered   here
nesting on   dried

dreaded

druid   word-scraps here

are

pupate   stories

pupil   stories

papal   stories

working to change

from one form

to another   here.

Out of   grammatic   chrysalides
grammar tic   chrysalides
the grammar of tics   chrysalides
the grammar of insect ticks   chrysalides
the grammar of Tourette tics chrysalides
grammatic   chrysalides emerge   tentative forms

fragile shapes

tender creatures

metaphors for   truth

not-truth.

The writing I do here is   exhaustively

extravagantly

exorbitantly

extremely

exceptionally

exasperatingly

excessive,

already-much-too-full, and approximately incomprehensibly elliptical, a spoken langue/tongue piece based on an intentionally outlandish and overwhelming form used by (some) conceptual, and POST poets (possibly, ill-defined, not by others, or else).

Really, this po-etic style is

innominate

anonymous

pseudonymous—

it is a babel, it is gibberish, it is a pidgined
tongueless alliterative confused glossolalia.
It is a plundering (Betts, 2005).
It is a sundering.
It is a thundering knuckle-undering wondering.

Avoiding the never-transparent academic language that inscribes the **offalic** and

violent taxonomy of

neo	liberal
neo	fascist
neo	conservative
knee	jerk
	education

(I long ago rejected "...the parade of

behaviorism, cognitivism, structuralism,

and neopositivism that have all failed to

study human activity successfully, in a way modeled after the assumedly cumulative, predictive, and stable natural sciences" (Lather, 2004, p.16), something that the good ole US of A **shootemup gummint** seems to have devoutly missed out on),

through a flagrantly and literally/littorally entirely tiresome, unspeakably visual and aural word conflagration, this po-etic begins to de-inscribe the nature of metaphoric, medicalized, ventriloquizing, normative discourse of social (scanty) science/education.

Why, you might ask? (Heh, thought ya never would). Well, dontcha know, "deconstruction is aimed at provoking fields into new moves and spaces where they hardly recognize themselves in becoming otherwise, the unforeseeable that they are already becoming" Lather, 2003, p. 5).

Pro voking   fields

pro vocal   feels

pro dding   meadows

pro domme   fiefdoms   into new

                                into gnu

moves   and   spaces

movies   &   spacecraft

moo visa   ampersand   time continuum

The chrysalides of knowledge. And
stuff. See.

It calls loudly, instead, through both its own fractured form and a florid/floral disordered peculiar deconstruction of spoken and written and labile word, and a discipline-busting redemption of gnu worried whored word-seeking flights of language fancy, for a disruption of language and all its piss-poor Neanderthalic representation in educational fallderall freefall. After all (thanks, Utah).

It   "...challenges neofascist state   apparatuses" (Denzin, 2003, p.258)—
                                                        the tools and machinery
                                                        the wrenches and equipment
                                                        the chutes and ladders
                                                        of out rageous global capitalist
                                                                rags to riches for some
                                                                just rags for most

Kulture

Kill zone.......

It seeks to   "...to empower the powerless and transform existing social inequalities and injustices" (McLaren, 1989, p. 160).

This pathetic poetic establishes the critical
ludicity/lucidity of textual practices and impractices
within slime-covered mime-slaughtered lime-
smothered mimetic education, delineating and
decircling the symphonic, sympathetic symbols of
Ed ducat shun stud-tease (Ed is who I call him,
that's not his name, his name has been changed to
protect   the innocent

the innocuous
the annihilated
the abhorred).

It asserts the importance of new langues, new tongues, new mouthings, new kinds of semiosis
halitosis, in both research re-certs and practice (makes perfect, makes prefect),

and   praxis
        axis
        axe sis
        give 'em   da axe da axe da axe
                        dioxin
                        da ozone

capitalist killing zone

          of the environment the world
that can more adequately represent the multiplicity (multiplication, division, a wonderful
new arithmetic calculus) of human experience and educational endangered endeavors.

This bathetic poetic, this bathmat of poetic, this bathosphere of rubber-ducky pomes, calls for an unkempt, disorderly (conduct), promiscuous, disagreeable ideology of representation, and inexplicably denounces, defines, and deinscribes through aural-visual whirled word art, the whored horrid wired weird word world of Ed ducat science ions, explicating the socio-cultural cult aphonic metaphors and floor mats of modernist Western shoot 'em up Clint Eastwood/John Wayne/Henry Fonda Ed ducat shun Zions.

(OMIGOD, CAN HE SAY THAT ON TELEVISION?)

Hell, it's only money anyway. That's what its all about, isn't it, really, the research dollars I gotta bring in, in order to meet some accountant's wet-dream of what tenure should lookie likey—if that's what they want, I can't play their game, have to

play sumpin' else, not
Monopoly, mebbe gin rummy.

the ideology   uv   education

the idiot logic   uv   ed DUCAT ion scanty

science
"...we grasp our lives in a narrative" (Taylor, 1989, p. 47).
we know the world through

sto	ries
shto (it means what, in Russian)	ries
what	rhizomes
what	risable zones
what	his/stories
what	her/stories
what	stores
	of knowledge
	of knowing
	of learning.

If we accept
    embrace
    wind our arms around and grasp
       the idea that the   correspondence theory of truth
                 the   correspondence school of epistemology
                 the notion and potion that words describe and denote a separate,
                 objective reality
   is no longer valid,

you're all with me on this one, right? correspondence theory of truth? 'member that one? the idea that there is a real world out there (somewhere, I dunno, over there to your left mebbe) and that it can be described outlined elicited delineated? the correspondence part comes in when you say that those words or that description CORRESPONDS to the real world, get it? and the idea that philosophers and other cool cats have scoped it all out that the way we do that is through language? and those groovy people have figgered in their nifty little way that language cannot, it's not possible, doesn't work like that, that language cannot

represent the world, it can only represent itself, see? WORDS ≠ WORLD, 'kay? It's all right there in the damn books, go read 'em yer own se'f (Gadamer, 1997; Putnam, 1988; Rorty, 1979; Smith, 1999b; 2006).

if we   denounce it
         depredate it
         dispute it
         deracinate it
         despise it
         destabilize it
if we   do the work of "troubling language as a transparent medium" (Lather, 2003, p. 5)
         then

"...it signals an end
to the only partly submerged goal
of language to master reality,
and it also sets language free
from that goal.
Language can then be explored
as another mode of existence.
Real in itself.
A different territory."
(Griffin, 1997, p. 218)

"Ethnographic knowledge refuses illusions of transparent reality… Its uses are potential rather than given…As an enactment of uncertainty and noncorrespondence to a "real," ethnography does not offer knowledge but demands thought" (Talburt, 2004, p. 98).

re	fuses	illusions
re	fracts	illusions
re	focuses	illusions

the fusion of illusion

Instead, we go around the corner and find

another metaphor
a trope
a turning of phrase

stretching by perspective
to a point we can't quite see.
We proceed down the stony way
between tall huts
that carve the air with spiring fists
built from piles of frozen metal
and burned powder
coalesced by magic
all facing square to the way.
On the other side
certain tired buildings look
in the wrong direction
laid up from huge bones collected and collated
across decades
arching over smoky fires
and covered with the outer skins
of giant beasts now dead
but that once surged across the ice.
In the centered space marches
a demon with white skin
and an angel with darkened robes
the two joined

at the loins
by a loose flap of parchment
and at the heads
by the writhing worms
of mercantile ideation.
The two in different languages speak
through interpreting devices of their own creation
and admire

      the stars
      the landscape
      the cackling horror.

Metaphor is quixotic
crepuscular
corrosive:
it eats away
at what we think
is the substance
of our lives
revealing deeper
more complex
minerals. $\left[\begin{smallmatrix} ? \\ . \end{smallmatrix} \right]$

Van Maanen said almost twenty years ago that "...the distinction between literature and science in ethnography is shrinking" (1988, p. x). A couple of years later, Stewart commented that "...ethnography is as much a literary as a scientific undertaking" (1989, p. 6).
And yet here we sit on our academic thrones almost two goldarn decades later writing mostly realist tales,   thinking they're the right thing,

> thinking that science is done one particular way (though some don't, some are arguing against it, e.g. (x.y.z.), Giangreco & Taylor, 2003; Lather, 2004; Lather & Moss, 2005; Maxwell, 2004).

        thinking they're the only thing
realist tales that still have a powerful hold on our
    (re)   presentation of
    (re)   search (Stephens, 2005).

Still, it is   a thing of writing
      a thing of imagination
      a thing of creation
      a thing of making.

For, "...culture is itself an interpretation... the results of ethnography are thus mediated several times over..." (Van Maanen, 1979, p. 549).

RE search   it is a making of culture
      over and over and over again
      made and remade
      making our bed
      culturing our bed
      and then   lying in it
                lying to it

RE search   is a writhing of culture
      it is a writing of culture
      it "words the world" (Lather, 2003, p.4)
      it is a kind of literature,   a storied fiction
                        a stoned friction
                        a stolen frictive

a stomped fiasco
a strangled fiend.

Fiction, did you know this, comes from a Latin verb meaning

to form or to make. Fact, did you know this, comes from a

Latin verb meaning to do. Research is a making, it is a doing,

it is a meaning making, it is a

doing of meaning, it is a kind of fact, it is a kind of

fiction.

"Intelligibility demands that language conform to hegemonic

and rigid hierarchies, systems of formulation, standards of

truth within a logic of solid mechanics" (Lather, 2004, p. 26).

But if you accept that the world is

not like that, then your research re(piss-poor)

presentation can not be like that. It starts to be, well, less,

uhmm, intelligible. More, ah, excessive. More like this.

"To encourage inquiry to create open texts that invite readers to
participate in the creation of meaning is to ask it to let go of its search
for certainty and certain purposes. Texts that exceed the boundaries
of what can be verified ask readers to take responsibility for thinking
through, with, and against research (Talburt, 2004, p. 95)."

This   poetic is a (huzzah)
       performance.   And: "...there is no distance between the performance
                            and the politics that the performance enacts. The two are
                            intertwined, each nourishing the other, opposite sides of
                            the same coin, one and the same thing." (Denzin, 2003,
                            p.258)

dis	po	etic
is	an	emic
dis	po	etic
is	po	litic

it is inescapable

it is ineluctable

it is elliptical

it is optical

it is deconstructive

it is unstable

it is critical

it is emotional

it is impractical

it is foolish

it is a bricolage

it is a flanage.

This poetic po(l)emic politic   resists

defies

contests

abjures

critiques   definition.

*

*
*
*
*
*
*
*
*
*
*
*
*
*
*
*
*
*
*

bottom line:

This po-litic po-etic calls for po-(l)emic recherché texts that are excessive+de-inscriptive.

what will this   performative

                        elliptical

                        excessive

                        writhing   be?

this ILL/ELLip(op)tical *po* – ETIC/EMIC/ **Lemic**/litic *po*st® thing

this writ(e)thing
will be a new utopic space for
knowing
understanding
meaning
making

it will be a place   where the margins are where the action is, rather than the center—an
                         undiscovered doughnut model of culture
it will be a place   where the razor-wired boundaries between archaic, burnt, lifeless
                         academic fields rust away, turning into new composted meaning-soil that
                         supports strange lush knowledge-meadows filled with a host of meaning-
                         making plantsandmammalsandinsectsandbirdsand
it will be a place   where the edges between meanings and understandings will be an
                         ecotonic edge of knowledge richness
it will be a place   where we are always coming-to-know

Poetics are at least   in part
                                    never in whole
                                                      about metaphors.
                                                      Metaphor "...is a tool of insight. It
                                                      provides us with a perspective for
                                                      comprehending something unknown by
                                                      comparing it to familiar objects and
                                                      experiences... metaphor is a heuristic device...
                                                      it leads to discovery..." (Pugh, Hicks, &
                                                      Davis, 1997, p. 18-19).
Just as the act of writing is a way of understanding the wor(l)d (Richardson, 1994), so too is
        the act of metaphor-making.
        The act of making   new metaphors
        stands on the shoulders of old metaphors
        deconstructing them in the process (Smith, 2001a).
META = change, a second-order.
PHOR = carry, bring.
                        carrying change
                        bringing second-order knowledge, understanding.
        Not just   a new   cultural cartography tool:
                      a whole new cultural cartography tool   CHEST
for exploring the marginalia   of the pages
                        off the pages of normate cultural maps.

◆　◆　◆

Deferences

Betts, G. (2005). Plunderverse: A cartographic manifesto. *Poetics.ca, 5* (n.p.). Retrieved from http://www.poetics.ca/poetics05/05betts.html

Busier, H.-L., Clark, K., Esch, R., Glesne, C., Pigeon, Y. & Tarule, J. (1997). Intimacy in research. *Qualitative Studies in Education, 10,* 165-170.

cummings, e.e. (1950/1997). *Xaipe.* NY: WW Norton Co.

Davis, L. (2002). *Bending over backwards: Disability, dismodernism & other difficult positions.* NY: New York University Press.

Denzin, N. (2003). Performing [auto] ethnography politically. *The Review of Education, Pedagogy, and Cultural Studies, 25,* 257–278.

Derrida, J. (1976). *Of grammatology.* Baltimore: Johns Hopkins Press.

Gadamer, H.-G. (1959/1988). On the circle of understanding. In J. Connolly & T. Kleutner (Eds. & Trans.), *Hermeneutics versus science? Three German views: Essays by H.-G. Gadamer, E.K. Specht, W. Stegmuller* (pp. 68-78). Notre Dame, In: University of Notre Dame Press.

Giangreco, M. & Taylor, S. (2003). "Scientifically based research" and qualitative inquiry. *Research & Practice for Persons with Severe Disabilities, 28,* 133-137.

Glesne, C. (1989). Rapport and friendship in ethnographic research. *International Journal of Qualitative Studies in Education, 2*(1), 45-54.

Glesne, C. (1997). That rare feeling: Re-presenting research through poetic transcription. *Qualitative Inquiry, 3*(2), 202-221.

Glesne, C. (1998). Ethnography with a biographic eye. In C. Kridel (Ed.), *Writing educational biography: explorations in qualitative research* (pp. 33-44). New York: Garland Publishing, Inc.

Glesne, C. (2003). The will to do: Youth regenerating community in Oaxaca, Mexico. *Educational Studies, 34,* 198-212.

Glesne, C. (2004). Tourist dollars. In G. Noblit, S. Flores, & E. Murillo (Eds.), *Postcritical Ethnography: Reinscribing Critique* (pp. 285-286). Cresskill, NJ: Hampton Press.

Glesne, C. (2006). *Becoming qualitative researchers: An introduction* (3rd ed.). New York: Longman.

Griffin, S. (1997). Ecofeminism and meaning. In K. Warren (Ed.) *Ecofeminism: Women, culture, nature* (pp. 213-226). Bloomington, Indiana: Indiana University Press.

Lather, P. (2003). Applied Derrida: (Mis)reading the work of mourning in educational research. Annual Meeting of the American Educational Research Association, Chicago, Il.

Lather, P. (2004). Scientific research in education: A critical perspective. *Journal of Curriculum and Supervision, 20*, 14-30.

Lather, P. & Moss, P. (2005). Introduction: Implications of the *Scientific Research in Education* report for qualitative inquiry. *Teachers College Record, 107*, 1-3.

Martin, P., & Glesne, C. (2002). From the global village to the pluriverse? 'Other' ethics for cross-cultural qualitative research. *Ethics, Place and Environment, 5*, 205-221.

Maxwell, J. (2004). Causal explanation, qualitative research, and scientific inquiry in education. *Educational Researcher, 33*(2), 3-11.

McLaren, P. (1989). *Life in schools: An introduction to critical pedagogy in the foundations of education.* NY: Longman.

Pugh, S. L., Hicks, J. W., & Davis, M. (1997). *Metaphorical ways of knowing: The imaginative nature of thought and expression.* Urbana, IL: National Council of Teachers of English.

Putnam, H. (1983). *Representation and reality.* Cambridge, MA: MIT Press.

Richardson, L. (1994). Writing: A method of inquiry. In N. Denzin & Y. Lincoln (Eds.), *Handbook of qualitative research* (pp. 516–529). Thousand Oaks, CA: Sage.

Rorty, R. (1979). *Philosophy and the mirror of nature.* Princeton, NJ: Princeton University Press.

Smith, P. (1999a). Food Truck's party hat. *Qualitative Inquiry, 5*, 244-261.

Smith, P. (1999b). Drawing new maps: A radical cartography of developmental disabilities. *Review of Educational Research, 69* (2), 117-144.

Smith, P. (2000). "I know how to do": Choice, control, and power in the lives of people with developmental disabilities. *Dissertation Abstracts International, 60* (11) A (University Microfilms No. 9951862).

Smith, P. (Oct. 2000). MAN.i.f.e.s.t.o.: A Poetics of D(EVIL)op[MENTAL] Dis{ABILITY}. Desegregating Disability Studies: An Interdisciplinary Conference, Syracuse, NY.

Smith, P. (2001a). Inquiry cantos: Poetics of developmental disability. *Mental Retardation, 39*, 379-390.

Smith, P. (2001b). MAN.i.f.e.s.t.o.: A Poetics of D(EVIL)op(MENTAL) Dis(ABILITY). *Taboo: The Journal of Education and Culture, 5* (1), 27-36.

Smith, P., & Godfrey, N. (June 2002). A Raucous, Hybrid Blues: Creating An Un/nerving Un/holy Entangled Alliance Between Whiteness Studies and Disability Studies. Second Annual Second City Conference on Disability Studies and Education, Chicago, IL.

Smith, P. (2004). The big problem with change. In G. Noblit, S. Flores, & E. Murillo (Eds.) *Postcritical ethnography: Reinscribing critique* (pp. 281-282).

Smith, P. (June 2006). a po – etic (poor not emic) uv ed DUCAT shun recherché repres(c)entation. Ethnography and Qualitative Research in Education Conference, Cedarville, OH.

Smith, P. (2006). Split------ting the ROCK of {speci [ES]al} e.ducat.ion: FLOWers of lang[ue]age in >DIS<ability studies. In S. Danforth & S. Gabel (Eds.) *Vital questions facing disability studies in education*. New York: Peter Lang.

Stephens, J. (2005). Beyond binaries in motherhood research. *Family Matters 69* (Spring-Summer), 88-93.

Stewart, J. (1989). *Drinkers, drummers, and decent folk: Ethnographic narratives of village Trinidad*. Albany, NY: State University of New York Press.

Talburt, S. (2004). Ethnographic responsibility without the "real". *The Journal of Higher Education, 75,* 80-103.

Taylor, C. (1989). *Sources of the self: The making of the modern identity*. Cambridge, MA: Harvard University Press.

Van Maanen, J. (1979). The fact of fiction on organizational ethnography. *Administrative Science Quarterly 24,* 539-550.

Van Maanen, J. (1988). *Tales of the field: On writing ethnography*. Chicago: University of Chicago Press.

Weathers, W. (1980). *An alternate style*. Rochelle Park, New Jersey: Hayden.

Chapter 7: This Closet

"We keep our true self (if there is such a thing) a secret and present to the world a plausible story." (Goodall, 2006, p. 189)

"There's no doubt about it, I was pretty crazy for a while there. I'm better now." (Varley, 1992, p. 471)

That's not true.
I mean, I was crazy.
But I'm not better now.
Different, maybe. But not better.
I'm still crazy (after all these—oh, never mind).
And I'm OK with that.
Lemme tell you about it.

*

This story is partly the story of a closet—
a real, not metaphoric, place to store clothing.
As I tell it, it is also the story of the metaphor
of my coming out of it
regarding parts of the story of my disability.
I tell only parts because the telling of the whole
is longer than this chapter will hold
and because a whole telling
involves writing the lives of others
that I believe I am bound to protect
(even though protecting some of them is not
what I want, what I need
given the ways that they've harmed me).
It is partial because I am partial—
not yet complete, not yet fully understood.

*

"I have discovered what I would have to call a soul, a part of myself I could never have imagined until one day, seven years ago, when hell came to pay me a surprise visit. It's a precious discovery. Almost every day I feel momentary flashes of hopelessness and wonder every time whether I am slipping. For a petrifying instant here and there, a lightning-quick flash, I want a car to run me over and I have to grit my teeth to stay on the sidewalk until the light turns green or I imagine how easily I might cut my wrists; or I taste hungrily the metal tip of a gun in my mouth; or I picture going to sleep and never waking up again. I hate those feelings, but I know that they have driven me to look deeper at life, to find and cling to reasons for living. I cannot find it in me to regret entirely the course my life has taken. Every day, I choose, sometimes gamely and sometimes against the moment's reason, to be alive. Is that not a rare joy?" (Solomon, 2001, p. 443)

*

This closet

    it's in a beat-up old farmhouse, built about 1873, the barn long

    since destroyed

    (though I built a new one, then walked away from it)

doesn't have a door

hasn't since before I bought the place.

There's no light in the closet, either—

I put things in, or take things out, more by feel than by sight.

The floor is made of the same wide pine boards

with which the rest of the bedroom is floored.

I know this

because I'm sitting on it right now

cross-legged

in the dark.

Its always dark, always night

not just because I'm sitting in a closet without a light

but because night is mostly the time that I'm awake.

    Night is black.

    Black and bleak are different in two ways:

    the letter e

    and the letter c.

    They are otherwise identical.

I'm sitting on the floor of this closet
in the dark
in the night
with my right ankle on top of my left thigh.
In my left hand is my pocket knife
the blade open.
I look at the knife—
though it is night and dark
there is a little light
from the moon coming in the window
on the other side of the bedroom
so I can see the knife—
I look at it, and, very carefully,
with as much precision as I can muster
I draw it across the skin on the side of my right ankle
just above the little knob of bone there.
The mark it makes is first a bit gray
and then reddens, and then leaks
the liquid I know will come.
The line on my skin is about an inch long.
I make one line.
And then another
parallel to it
about half an inch above.
That line reddens and leaks in the same way.
And then a third, above the other two.
It is a kind of I Ching hexagram
written in the blood of my body.
Perhaps if I knew its meaning
I could tell something of the future.
My future.
I look at the marks, watching them bleed.
I feel some small physical pain
but really, the sensation is nothing.

                        Nothing at all.
                        Nothing
compared to the   deep and
                            abiding and
        terrible   blackness of soul and heart
that engulfs my entire body
that has blossomed like some   internal
        unseen
        viral monster
come to eat up and suck out all   meaning and
                                     life and
        sensation except: darkness.
Blackness.
Bleakness.
Indescribable terror and horrible, horrible soul-pain.

                                                *

I'm crazy.
More specifically, I'm batty. Deranged. Gone around the bend.
Berserk. Loony. Dotty. Mental. Lunatic.
Cracked up. Insane. Psycho.
Bonkers. Fallen off the deep end. Raving. Daft.
Loco. Demented. Touched.
Nuts. Disturbed. Loopy.
Lost his marbles. Screwy. Unhinged.
Whacked.
Completely and totally bugjob.
Mad, so the saying goes, as a hatter.

                                                *

The first time I went to jail
because of this pain
I sat in the back of a police cruiser
handcuffs wrapped too-tightly around my wrists
holding my arms behind me against the backseat
on an otherwise wonderful, blue and sunny, mid-summer day.

The car raced across half the width of the state
in just a few short minutes.
The officer listened to country music,
talked on his cell phone, and
ignored the police radio.
They looked in all the holes of my body
took away my belt, my shoelaces.
In a holding cell, I sat on a stainless steel bench
watching a black man sleep
on another bench on the far wall.
After six hours, someone brought cash for bail
and I left.
The black man continued to sleep.

*

You can look me and my silly little symptoms up in the DSM *IV (TR)*.
That's the *Diagnostic and Statistical Manual of Mental Disorders Fourth Edition
(Text Revision)* to you, sport.
My symptoms make up a diagnosis, a label, a thing to be called.
The thing has a number:
296.3.
Major Depression Recurrent.
Recurrent means it happens over and over.
Here's what it says:

"A. Five (or more) of the following symptoms have been present during the same 2-week
period and represent a change from previous functioning; at least one of the symptoms is
either (1) depressed mood or (2) loss of interest or pleasure...
(1) depressed mood most of the day, nearly every day, as indicated by either subjective report
(e.g., feels sad or empty) or observation made by others (e.g., appears tearful)...
(2) markedly diminished interest or pleasure in all, or almost all, activities most of the day,
nearly every day (as indicated by either subjective account or observation made by others)
(3) significant weight loss when not dieting or weight gain (e.g., a change of more than 5% of
body weight in a month), or decrease or increase in appetite nearly every day.
(4) insomnia or hypersomnia nearly every day

(5) psychomotor agitation or retardation nearly every day (observable by others, not merely subjective feelings of restlessness or being slowed down)

(6) fatigue or loss of energy nearly every day

(7) feelings of worthlessness or excessive or inappropriate guilt (which may be delusional) nearly every day (not merely self-reproach or guilt about being sick)

(8) diminished ability to think or concentrate, or indecisiveness, nearly every day (either by subjective account or as observed by others)

(9) recurrent thoughts of death (not just fear of dying), recurrent suicidal ideation without a specific plan, or a suicide attempt or a specific plan for committing suicide...

C. The symptoms cause clinically significant distress or impairment in social, occupational, or other important areas of functioning...

Recurrent

A. Presence of two or more Major Depressive Episodes.

> **Note**: To be considered separate episodes, there must be an interval of at least 2 consecutive months in which criteria are not met for a Major Depressive Episode..."

*

I was eighteen the first time I tried to kill myself.
I took some pills.
Looking back on it, I didn't put everything I had into it.
Kind of half-hearted.
I remember talking on the telephone in my parents' bedroom.
I felt quiet, calm. Relaxed.
I remember thinking to myself: Finally. It's done.
I can take THAT off the list of things I need to do.

*

I shopped for a therapist.
I didn't know what a good one looked like.
But I knew it when they weren't good.
One psychologist diagnosed me with this.
Another claimed I had that.
This therapist said I should do these.
That therapist said I should do those.
I finally met one who made sense to me

(although the psychiatrist I went to
said she made no sense at all).
A social worker, we met in her living room
every week for a year
she in one corner, me in another.
A big soft red easy chair
with a floor lamp and low shelf of books nearby.
After months of talking
I asked her what I should do.
She said, "You already know what to do."
She was right
and I knew it—knew it before I asked the question—
knew it before she answered it—
though I didn't want to admit it
didn't want to do it
was afraid to—terrified that if I did
there would be nothing else.
Afraid to admit the mistake I had made two years before.
When finally there was no choice—
me kneeling on the wide pine floor boards of the long, narrow kitchen, sobbing—
when there were no other options—
I did what had to be done, should have never needed to be done.
Later, when she asked me, "Why did you do it?"
I asked her back, "What other choice did I have?"

                                                            *

Is the label who I am?
Is that my identity?
Are the things they call symptoms—
are those the meaning of my life?
If they aren't, where do I draw the line
(like the knife, on the skin
above my ankle)
between who I think I am as a person
and the words they use to describe me

(the words that make me not a person
but a thing, an object, an it)?
Is the thing that they make me be
by the words they use to describe me —
is that the true me?
Is the me that I think I am —
is that just another symptom
another manifestation of my sickness, my disease?

                                                    *

My psychiatrist's office is on the second floor
of an old and handsome Victorian house
on upper Main Street. Pale yellow, with white trim.
Inside are wood floors, varnished wood trim, high ceilings.
There is no waiting room
just chairs and a table at one end of the hall
near a window that looks out over the street.
I never know if I'm supposed to wait there before going into his office.
I always do.
He always comes out and calls me in.
He doesn't have a secretary.
He calls me in and asks me about the drugs he has prescribed.
That's what psychiatrists do, now, is prescribe drugs.
He has thick white hair, and glasses, is clean-shaven.
He is calm and quiet while he asks me about the drugs.
The first time, he gave me free samples
like the grocer who used to give me candy
when my mother and I went shopping.
He asks me about the drugs and then it starts.
The therapy. The part where he uses words to make me—
better.
He shouts at me.
Really, shouting.
He yells.
He's enraged.

Very, very angry.

At me.

His face is red. His eyes, glaring. His mouth is pinched. He sweats.

He puts his face close to mine and screams at me.

Startled, I pull my head back.

Can people in other offices in the building hear this?

I remember thinking:

is this what therapy with psychiatrists is supposed to be like?

*

Le Guin (1991) talks about being afraid "to lie down and fall black" (p. 69).

And that to think about the black makes it come.

The thing I remember most about the bad times

is the darkness.

It was everywhere, in everything.

It is everywhere, in everything.

Waiting. To come out. To take over, engulf.

Not a fog, or miasma.

Instead, it is a taking away of lumination.

Its not just that there was—is—no light; it was—is—a literal, physical presence.

An object you could pick up. A metaphor.

Everything that occurred, happened at night. There was no day.

In the bad times,

even when there is day, there is only the darkness.

*

The second time I went to jail

I rode in a van, handcuffs attached to a leather belt around my waist.

They took me in front of my daughter

who cried out when they said

why they had come.

The cell was four feet by six feet

three walls concrete, one wall bars

that opened up to face another concrete wall.

Along one side was a metal bed, a foam mattress covered with plastic.

At one end was a toilet: a hole in the concrete floor

with a roll of paper next to it.
I lay on the bed all night
listening to someone yelling,
another vomiting.
Breakfast was two pieces of toast soggy with butter
and a single cup of bad coffee.
Mid-morning, a man (I had known him in another life)
came and asked me some questions, and went away.

*

The darkness came when I was 14, one night.
An animal arrived—not my fault.
I remember circling the house
walking in the grass, over and over
head up towards the stars, looking south
facing Blackman's Hill
and then north, towards Tanner's Pond
howling, silently.
No sound.

*

Gravity sucks.
It pulls my body down
relentlessly, ruthlessly, mercilessly.
Gravity is made entirely of extraordinary sadness
and its job is to ensure that I do not get up
do not ever rise.
It is an invisible force that grabs my neck
and pushes my body down to the ground.
It makes me sleep for 14 hours, 16 hours
at a time.
It makes me give up eating.
It makes me give up thinking.
It makes me give up feeling.
Gravity wants me laid out,
spread-eagled, pinned down.

It lets me up to put on a little show
of what it means to be a person
a few moments every day
for the women, for the children
for the neighbors and the bosses and the colleagues
so that I (and so that they)
can pretend that everything is alright
can pretend that everything will be OK.
And then the show is over.
Making breakfast or doing laundry
or going shopping or
simply
smiling.
The show is over and I can go
back to doing what gravity wants.

*

The darkness came next
the time when I lived in a barn.
And then again
when I lived in the log cabin.
No one knew. I kept it hidden.
It seemed important to keep it hidden.
Even from myself.
Really, I didn't know it was there
until much later—many years later
and only realized it, looking back
seeing it again with fresh eyes
recognizing the signs.
Yes. I see it now. Yes.

*

I went back to the psychiatrist.
Really, you ask? Why would you do such a thing?
I decided that I didn't want to take the drugs anymore.
It wasn't just that they weren't doing any good.

It was also because they were doing active harm.

Causing other, um, symptoms. And I knew

that if I tried to get off of them

on my own

without a plan to slowly get off of them

doing that would make it all worse.

So I went to him, and asked him to help me get off of them.

He looked at me.

He got up, said, "I'll be back," and left.

I waited. He was gone

a long time. I didn't know why. I don't know now.

He finally came back, sat down. Didn't look at me.

"You shouldn't stop taking them," he said. "You shouldn't come

back, anymore, either. I can't help you. There's nothing I can do for you."

I waited.

Silence. He didn't say anything more. Shuffled and wrote on some papers.

    I got up and walked out.

    (I went to my general practitioner, and asked for help to

    set up a plan to get me off the drugs. He looked in some books,

    wrote some prescriptions, told me how long to stay on what drugs,

    at what strength, how to slowly reduce the amounts, told me

    to call him if I had any problems. It worked. I haven't taken

    them for 9 years.)

*

I worked once for a state bureaucracy

in a couple of different roles

out of a couple of different offices in a state complex.

The complex consisted of a set of large brick buildings

built around the turn of the twentieth century

the state hospital for people said to have psychiatric disabilities.

The buildings were connected with each other

by a fairly complex system of underground tunnels

so it was possible to travel throughout the complex

without going above ground.

Off of several of these tunnels were a set of locked rooms
which at the time I worked there were used for storage.

One of the offices I worked out of
was on the third floor of the building.
The office suite was one wing of that floor
and consisted of two long hallways
at right angles to each other.
The hallways intersected at a large room
(then used as a collective work room)
off of which was a sun porch
enclosed on three sides with large windows.
The porch was used, when I worked there, as a meeting space.

My own office was about 6 feet wide
and ten feet long.
It had a single window at one end.
At the other end was a metal door
with a six inch by six inch window in it.
The walls were concrete block.

As I worked there
I began to realize
that it was likely that the space I called an office
was the living space for someone
possibly for many years
when it was part of the mental hospital.
This person would have spent most days
on the sun porch, or the large room
which was probably what was then called a day room.

I came to understand
that the side rooms off of the tunnels connecting the buildings
were places where particularly violent

so-called patients
lived.
They would have been completely out of sight
of most visitors to the complex.

At one corner of the complex
was the last remaining portion of what was
even when I worked there
the State Mental Hospital.
It was completely surrounded by high fences
topped with razor wire.
There was only one door
through which someone could enter the facility.
It was publicly described as a place
for people alleged to have committed crimes
to undergo so-called forensic psychiatric evaluations
and that these evaluations typically required people
to live there for no more than 30 days or so.
I came to understand, however
that there were a number of people living in the facility
who had been living there for many decades
and about whom it was said by long-term politicos
in the state bureaucracy
that they would never leave the facility alive.

As I worked in the complex
I began to realize that in another time
the space that I used as an office
might have been my home.
Given the story that I've told here
in some ways its a kind of miracle
that I managed to stay outside the razor-wired walls
of the so-called hospital.

*

How much of this is real
I wonder?
How much have I made up?
How much is fiction, how much is fact?
How much have I kept hidden to protect myself?
How much have I kept hidden from myself?
How much can I tell, and still be safe?
Who can I tell, and still be safe?

                                                                        *

I have spoken as if it was all in the past tense.
As if it was something that was already done, finished.
Complete.
Over with.
That, of course, is not true.
It is always here, always becoming, always present.
It never goes away.
It doesn't know how.
And I wouldn't know what to do without it.
I don't know what to do without it.

                                        ♦   ♦   ♦

References

Goodall, H. (2006). *A need to know: The clandestine history of a CIA family.* Walnut Creek,
      CA: Left Coast Press.

Le Guin, U. (1991). *Searoad: Chronicles of Klatsand.* NY: Harper Collins Publishers.

Solomon, A. (2001). *The noonday demon: An atlas of depression.* NY: Scribner.

Varley, J. (1992). *Steel beach.* NY: G.P. Putnam's Sons.

Chapter 8: BEyon|ce|D inclusion: Wud mite[ymose] be NEXTERATED X

Here's the thing, see.

I'm the inclusion guy.

You know, that one teacher at the high school—the curmudgeonly, flakey, progressive special educator—who's all into including students with disabilities into general education. Pushin' the principal to get kids into chemistry class, or English class, or whatever. Kids with intellectual/developmental disabilities. Kids with severe reputations. Kids "on the spectrum." Kids who are just way out there.

I worked in schools and in agencies providing support to people with disabilities in the community, for years. Now I'm the inclusion guy at the university. That one guy—the curmudgeonly, flakey, progressive education professor—who's all into helping educators understand how to include students with disabilities in general education. Pushing my colleagues to teach their pre-service teachers how to make that happen.

I am a self-described pain in the ass. I admit it. Wrote a book about it (Smith, 2010). (Inclusion, that is, not bein' a pain in the ass.)

But I've been thinkin' lately (perfessers do that kinda thing, ya know?). What if a goal of inclusion—across oppressions and identities—is not a useful trajectory for this thing we call education? What if the

Western
White
Eurocentric
Neoliberal
Institutionalization

support(hose)ing the   dominant

      demonic   moneysucking—

1. 3 trillion dollar (Strauss, 2013a)

(globally $4.4 trillion and growing REALLY fast)

(Strauss, 2013b)—

industrial facade

that we pretend iz

teaching/learning
is so deeply   flawed

                                         corrupted

                                         broken

                                         crippled

                                         mutilated

                                         injured

                                         dismembered

                                         defective   ABLEIST METAPHORS IN TENSION

ALLY DEPLOYED TO HIGH BRIGHT THE LIGHT OF DAY THARE COMMON/CON MAN USE IN

INSTITUTIONALLY ABLE EST COMMODIFIED WESTERNIZED (WHY AT URP) KULCHUH (SHOCK

ELECTROAD)

that applying values and strategies of inclusion to   it,

('cause   it

really is an   it

                              a thing,

                              an objet (not d'art)

                              a   reified

commodified

bona fide

crapified

Fid (oh)

dog of a corrupt capitalist imperialist)

is like applying a patch {adams} to the blown out|up bicycle tire inner toob of
      edoo[doo]cashinal   infra

                                                               infro

                                                               infree (alley ally ahlee)

                                                                                    structure

that is already   wholly

                   holy

                   holely   totally

                              escalatingly

absolut(vodka)(kafka)e/loot (yeah, stolen from us all)/ludic ly

broken? Hell, not just broken, but weaponsuvmassdeconstruction nuked into total

Hicks
(hickey)
boson boatswain particle(board) capitalist annihilation. Nukified fried Kentucky Colonel
Fred Sanders antivegetarianist salmonellaed bloodied .edu cash national
chicken
chick (Barbie and) Ken
Education is a burned-out hulk (not green, but certainly a blue-eyed monster) flagrantly
fragrantly vagrantly conflagration
                                   flagellation
that we have been   conned   out   of
                              conned   in   to
                              conning   towered toward to word.
                                                 we all live in a yellow…
Worse: what if the tiny and huge storeez we (Ma)tell° about inklu(e)shun and op(ed)press on
(sticker) and eduKAT(E)scion are told from the totally privileged, centered, and dominant
minority, surrounded by (butt still totally dominating) the grassrooted/margined/edged/
boundaried/segregated majority?
This   piece
(not peace or peas or kale)
               uv writhing writing witch yoo(hoo) are weeding reeding cums to you from a
          place
that I have most very precisely and pretty much exquisitely inexactly already de/inscribed
befour, undt zo if ewe wanna know how you landed in this patch of doo-doo doing(Loch)
(lox)ness, go two/four/up/by (Smith, 2001a) and (Smith, 2001b) and (Smith, 2006) and
(Smith, 2008) for a
          de/entailed
          derailed
          entrailed {studying thereof tea leaves fer a prediction uv da foochur}
          dental tool (suffering the pain of THAT hole ting)
TRANS(embodied sexool)mogrif(ter)(mast)ication fornication
er, ok, storee
aboud wut dis iz and hough ya mighta landerated on this partic(ell)ular(loid) molar
planet(al)oid. It enters hear (exit only) from "the spring of the imagination, when the winter
of clean positivism fades completely and we are fre/er/iere" (Zach Richter, personal

communication, April 25, 2013). Accept, of course, positivism wud never clean, not even by the Tide® of manufactured epistemofflogical ocean of Comte and his followers (and, for good measure, fuck you, Foucault).

In sum (quotient and equationally eloquent elegance), waddle happen(stance now) here will be an en|in-tire\less/ly trans=crossdressing=gressive, neuroqueered(un)iversive|aversive, and already-much-too-contrarian, in|un|at|tentionally (tenHUT!), oppositional, abolitional

u/eu/dystopic
dye st(r)op(t)ic
die, sucker!
di-succor
hopic
elliptic
marked/marketed

textual
text you all
Tex-Mex dual duel

anarchic (not arched) ick ick ick writing wry thing un|en|door|dour|jam—peach—bed thing(iemabob)(nod Jack) is not   metaphoric
me 2 flower lick

it is embodied and imbedded and has been bedded (a beast wid 2 approxiMATE backs) and lived (to tell the tall tell-tail tale tee(hee) beer) and in terrupt/terrogate the world and how it is con/de (Rice) structed.

LIVE, FROM NEW YORK, IT'S SATUR

nalia made gnu -   -   -   -   -   -   -   -   -   -   -

And, in doo-wing sew, I yam (potatoes arise!) committed (asylumed) "to language as a site of experimentation, power, struggle, and hope" (Giroux, 2012, p. 100), though probabbley NOT exactly in the way ole Henry had in mind (though with luck and hard work, the outcome will be along the lines of what he intended).

Here, I always already

critique the   creation
          consumption
          cooption
          commercialization

commodification
consorbtion   of   inclusive
                                      universalist
                                      eugenicist
                                      monocultural
                                      education

from the place of the counter-hegemonic neurodiverse|queer polyculture.

Why?

Or, moh bettuh:

Wry?

Here's the thing: "It is generally accepted that 'Inclusion' means inviting those who have been historically locked out to 'come in'. …Who has the authority or right to 'invite' others in?" (Asante, 2013).

Well, Nobodaddy (Heh. Because, of course, Secresy gains females loud applause).

They that do are self-authorizing and demonic.

The act of inclusion by the White
                              middle/upperclass
                              male
                              heterosexual
                              able-bodied (however temporar(e)olee)
                              positivist
                              Eurocentric
                              northern

                                                            dominating
                                                            hegemonic
                                                            rule-enforcing
                                                            monosemic

of all dem poh liddle udders

reinforces the rights and power uv da self-per(de)ceiving do-gooder domination nation neoconlibs without changing a goddam thing.

whoo maid dem so special and exalted and almighty as to let ebberbody else in?

and wry is id dat ebberbody else wantz to get in|en|em bed widdim anyway? doesn't that make us

        com

im

ex   plicit wid da ting{aling} dat deyve maid? like wee wanna bee part(y) uv dat

anyhoo?   I don't think

so.

dat be evil incarnate (whether perceived or nut).

And, well, see, er, **MORE:**

"One of the problems with the move to 'promoting inclusion' is that inclusion in practice

implicitly assumes that the quality of mainstream society is not only desirable, but

unproblematic and legitimate. . . . Equally, a fundamental, if implicit, premise of social

inclusion is the existence of an 'ideal of common life'... which everyone should aspire to. In

practice this assumes a general consensus on basic values around involvement in community,

work, family and leisure.... In addition, social inclusion discourse implies that society is

comprised of a comfortable and satisfied 'included majority' and a dissatisfied 'excluded

minority'. This focuses attention on the excluded minority and fails to take seriously the

difficulties, conflicts and inequalities apparent in the wider society which actually generate

and sustain exclusion ..." (Spandler, 2007, p. 6)

I question with ex(ice)   treme

                             dream

                             cream

 pre[post]judice the desirability (ah, sweet desire!) and legit|ext|int|imacy of that (this)

thesethosethem society—its more than a little   problematic

                                                conblemishauto[matic]

                                                fanatic

There is, indeed, a much-too-already-comfy|cuddly|cushy dominating hegemonic hierarchical

uber-class   supported and

                extended and

                amplified and

                boosted and

                accelerated

by an absolootly ginormous disparity of wealth (Domhoff, 2013) and income (Wiseman,

2013), da biggerest on this (or probably any other) planet, one that is creating

                          "difficulties, conflicts and inequalities"

(those words are much too weak/dainty/flimsy to describe what is in fact in place, but let 'em

serve [eat cake] for now). This awl plaize out[house] in an e—ducat—(sc)ionall {solar} system dat is "dominated by pedagogies that are utterly instrumental and geared toward memorization, conformity, and high-stakes test taking ... intellectual dead zones and punishment centers" (Giroux, 2012, p. 117) (a-gun, dese wurds do nod be-gun

> to do
> to be
> or not ornate
> do be do be do

justice to the annihilation
> obliteration
> amputation

of hope, equity, and democracy that might possibly have beginnerated to go{o} on there—but let 'em serve(ice) fer now).

In such a sizdem (modeled on biznez), the best we can even marginally hope for is to include "students who will undoubtedly be viewed as, for want of any other term, artificial transplants whose ersatz presence in the general education classroom will inevitably be subject to abiding doubts about their assimilative adequacy" (Gallagher, 2010, p. 36). Witch just ain't good enough.

Nod fer da crips and queers dat I hang wid. Me and mine(d).

Given the screwed-uppedness (that's a technical term, they teach it to ya in doctor school, all others need not apply) of our increasingly privatized (the balls of it)

.edu cash nationalism

> sizdem
> size [not]dem-ocratic
> size DOES matter

undt da   horrors
> whores
> errors

that it is   perpetrating
> decimating
> segregating
> desolating
> regulating
> detonating
> perpetuating
> devastating

on our|my|the   culture—on our polyculture   (Aronowitz, 2008; Giroux, 2012; Illich, 1971; Prakash & Esteva, 2008).

We need to stop working towards inclusion, because including people with disabilities into the broken and harmful institution of education doesn't make sense. Instead, as Illich said, we need to figure out what it might mean to "deschool" society—to imagine and create a way for children and adults, in this silly culture within which we find ourselves, to learn and grow and teach and change in ways based on common sense, as Prakash and Esteva say... I think that is the real work. We need to be focused on a bigger, more important, more radical and revolutionary project. (Smith, 2013, pp. 275–276)

My colleagues and friends and teachers and co-conspirators in the neurodiversity movement have taught me sum tings   though not always explicitly and I be tinkin' many uv 'em wood arguate wid me, which I
TOTALLY relish {and mustard}.

One of 'em is this:

                              Inclusion cannot be given.

Whoah.   Dig on that, Jack.
                 Inclusion~power.
Perhaps   inclusion=power.
        And "real power can not be given, only taken" (Coppola, 1990). In da zame weigh, reel
        inkylooseshun
        ion from Zion
cannot be gibbon, only taken, bacon. This taking of inclusion—leads us call it the
part(whole)ic°ip(le)ation in the common [core] zoshial and gultural-gluteous cotton fabric of
greater and lesser humanic communities—
(and by this, dear reader, I do not mean "a 19th-century notion of a homogenous, tight-knit
and small locale" (Ben-Moshe, 2011, p. 195), uh uh, nosirreebob, Bud (this one's fer) rather a
plaize of "support and acceptance ... based on solidarity and unity ... the antithesis of
confinement" (Ben-Moshe, 2011, p. 196))
involves
devolves
revolves

necessarily a clam chowduh claim to the active|not-passive|perseverative in-de-re-volv{o}ement in the politea of disdatdemdese(bull)dozerhoser communities, and a flame[thrower] claim (sometimes re-claim) to powuh (to da peepul).

My homies in da neurodiver[ticulosis]gent (should be femme) activism and scholarship claim their|our right to be who they|we are and who they|we want to be in a not-yet-our-culture-because-it-hasn't-entirely-been-created-or-imagined,

perseverating (over and over and over and over and over and over)

> flapping (rejoice, you wrigglers!)
> squeeeeeeeeeeeealing
> echoing echoing echoing echoing echoing

Can you gimme an amen, brothers and sisters?

our way into a GNU corpogoddamnreality that rejects da

> pure-snow-white honkey strait|straight bourgeois subdude BORING
>> whatever you wanna call what it is we got now.

Like, fuck DAT shit, know w'am sayin'? Heh.

Anarchoneuroqueer and owning/celebrating/claiming it. And through that ownership/celebration/claiming, creating a radical youtopia(ry)n vision (deaf and)

> of what will cum:

"the aspiration is to fundamentally change the way we react to each other, the way we respond to difference or harm, the way normalcy is defined and the ways resources are distributed and accessed" (Ben-Moshe, 2011, p. 359).

Da werk, mein freund, den, is dis:

end the pederasstized sozial insTITooshun of .edu cash nationalism globalisation as we know id. Create Samsung knew in its (bed)stead, preferably(oblate) samsara dat Duz da saim tingaling as an institution but is not institootshun[Big]Al. Do so across all levels, most especially at the level of so-called higher (I wanna, I wanna, I wanna, I wanna take you) education.

In this cultural space, money cannot possibly be involved.

I have absofuckinglutely no ideer (in da headlights) what this space (the final frunteer) looks like or smells like or tastes like or how to make it happenin', Jackson. Only that it needs to.

But the cool (totally frigid[aire]) thingking is, see, that eye donerated half (or three-quarters) to

> know

sow

blow

GO!

what it loogs lige, matey. This is not some kinda hocus pocus locus, hear (me out and back in the screen door of somnambulant justusice), nossuh; it's not some weird wired whored buncha (prolly pot, huh) smoke and freak show mirrors (here's lookin' at you, kid). As Ben-Moshe points out, the abolitionists didn't have a clew (sailing along) what an Amurrican   soziety
coquettery

without slavery would look like, only that slavery must end. They made it up as they went along.

Wee can do da zame.

When weave finisherated, if we ged id (w)right, whether we're (w)rong or right, whether we're wroing, we won't even have to conceeve of

the

strange

ting

we call

inclusion.

♦   ♦   ♦

References

Aronowitz, S. (2008). *Against schooling: For an education that matters.* Boulder, CO: Paradigm.

Asante, S. (2013). What is inclusion? *Inclusion Network.* Retrieved from www.inclusion.com/inclusion.html

Ben-Moshe, L. (2011). *Genealogies of resistance to incarceration: Abolition politics within deinstitutionalization and anti-prison activism in the U.S.* Retrieved from ProQuest Digital Dissertations. (UMI No. 3495084).

Coppola, F. (Director) (1990). *The godfather: Part III* [Motion picture]. United States: Paramount Pictures.

Domhoff, G. (2013). Wealth, income, and power. Retrieved from http://www2.ucsc.edu/whorulesamerica/power/wealth.html

Gallagher, D. (2010). Educational researchers and the making of normal people. In C. Dudley-Marling & A. Gurn (Eds.). *The myth of the normal curve* (pp. 25–38). New York: Peter Lang.

Giroux, H. (2012). *Education and the crisis of public values: Challenging the assault on teachers, students, and public education.* New York: Peter Lang.

Illich, I. (1971). *Deschooling society.* New York: Harper & Row.

Prakash, M., & Esteva, G. (2008). *Escaping education: Living as learning within grassroots culture.* New York: Peter Lang.

Smith, P. (2001a). Inquiry cantos: A poetics of developmental disability. *Mental Retardation, 39*, 379–390.

Smith, P. (2001b). MAN.i.f.e.s.t.o.: A Poetics of D(EVIL)op(MENTAL) Dis(ABILITY). *Taboo: The Journal of Education and Culture, 5*(1), 27–36.

Smith, P. (2006). Split------ting the ROCK of {speci [ES]al} e.ducat.ion: FLOWers of lang[ue]age in >DIS<ability studies. In S. Danforth & S. Gabel (Eds.), *Vital Questions in Disability Studies in Education* (pp. 31–58). New York: Peter Lang.

Smith, P. (2008). an ILL/ELLip(op)tical *po* – ETIC/EMIC/**Lemic**/litic *post*® uv ed DUCAT ion *re*cherché *re*pres©entation. *Qualitative Inquiry, 14*, 706–722.

Smith, P. (Ed.) (2010). *Whatever happened to inclusion? The place of students with intellectual disabilities in education.* New York: Peter Lang.

Smith, P. (2013). Looking to the future. In P. Smith (Ed.), *Both sides of the table:*

Autoethnographies of educators learning and teaching with/in [dis]ability
(pp. 263–277). New York: Peter Lang.

Spandler, H. (2007). From social exclusion to inclusion? A critique of the inclusion imperative   in mental health. *Medical Sociology Online, 2*(2), 3–16.

Strauss, V. (2013a, January 9). Education reform as a business. *Washington Post.* Retrieved from

    http://www.washingtonpost.com/blogs/answer-sheet/wp/2013/01/09/education-reform-as-a-business/

Strauss, V. (2013b, February 9). Global education market reaches $4.4 trillion—and is growing. *Washington Post.* Retrieved from http://www.washingtonpost.com/blogs/answer-sheet/wp/2013/02/09/global-education-market-reaches-4-4-trillion-and-is-growing/

Wiseman, P. (2013, September 10). Top 1 percent collected record share of U.S. household income in 2012. iPolitics. Retrieved from http://ipolitics.ca/2013/09/10/top-1-percent-collected-record-share-of-u-s-household-income-in-2012/

Chapter 9: ~~[wo]mani**FEST**[ival][the big]O~~ n*eu*roq*ue*er: nodes fer uh Grammuh C

1.

neuroqueer.

neu   roq   ueer.

new   rock   uhr.

neuro queer.

neuro queer. ya   hear?

neuro queer. ya   here?

          we're hier   (not archy)

          in da blogosphere

    makin'   a new grammar.

2.

see, dere's a Grammar A (Weathers, 1980). Dat's da grammar uv white people   priv   leged

                                                                    privy   ledged

                                                                    shit   rocks

old white dead men   upper   class

                          dey ain't got no   class

                          dey don't have to

                          dey above all dat, knowutmsayin?

                          head uv da   class

                          dey above da   class

                          dey da ony   class

                          dey de FINE da   class

                          dey create da   class

                          deys n mein   class

                                      class   ic

                                        class   ick
                                        icky   poo
                                        ick   shit

stan   dard   english
the   language that made the   r-word
the   langue
the   tongue
            slidin' around, slippery
            in they mouth
            leering, ogling, staring
                                    eng   lish
                                    ing   lish
            tongue of white people
            tongue of privilege
            tongue of power
            tongue of   control   ling   us
                            ing   lish
                        controlling   us
            locking   us   up
            lock   king   us   down
            lock   queen   us   in   back   wards
            lock   cock   us   outta da   fore   ground
            lock   cunt   us   into da   out   side

eng   lish
ang   uish
ang   lish
the langue of the Angles
the langue that made   right   angles
                and   str8ght   lines

            no room for queer   lines
                         bent   lines

                    out   lines
                    out   liers
                                        these cannot be
        imagined
              drawn   (and quartered)
              painted   in Grammar A.

Grammar A is the grammar   of   binary
                          of   het
                          of   two dimensions
                          of   a single Euclidian plane that while
        extending   forever

                                        goes   nowhere

3.
see, dere's a Grammar B (Weathers, 1980).   dis da grammar
                                        grandmudder
                                              uv   hipsters
                                                    cool cats
                                                    hot sax

        bits   and
        pieces   and
        fragments   and
        parts   and

it repeats itself
it repeats itself
it repeats itself
it repeats itself   and others   little complex loops forward and back

sentences that go nowhere sidewise around and around and around painting circles and songs
and stories and pomes about the day and night in counter-hegemonic dialects, mixing it up
messing it up messinwidit

Grammar B is da grammar uv   exploration
                                   finding the edges
                                   discovering the boundaries
                                   describing the margins
                                                        but   it remains binary
                                                                it remains het
                                                                it remains planar
it understands the edges of the plane, may even live there, but does not go beyond
it remains caught up in the   meaning-making
                                   meaning-receiving
                                          of the given structures of the   dominant
                                                                             dominating
                                                                                  hegemony.

4.
Now Grammuch C, see, dats a hole new ting.
Neurodiverse
Neuro two verse
Neuro three pome
Neo rhizomatic {who} we are
                    creates da   Grammuh C
                                   Gramercy (Park)
                                   grant mercy on we see
                                   granmudder sea   (great ocean waves
             huge tsunamis
             crawling across da   world
                                   whirled
                                   wired, weird
                                   word)
Grammuh C, se[a]e,   under
                 over   stands
                        sits
                        knows

"   "

like no udder grammah dat   the politics of the flesh are the roots of power

(Le Guin, 1995, p. 158).

neurodiversity makes Grammah C.
creates it.
builds it.
speaks it.
          da gnu wurd.
          a noo langue.
          a nui tongue, slipping slowly and cairfully ovar sweet new flesh.   licking
                                                                                      licking

this Grammah C   iz outside da margins
                   off da map
nah: dey iz no map
                            it works
                            it feels
                            it loves
                                              in three dimensions
nah: in more: a multiverse
                                                           the polyverse
                                                           a poly amorous verse

          uh many imagined   cross
                             inter
                             trans
                                    not one
                                    not da udder
                                    nod   even inbuhtween
                                           odd
                                                      but a gnu notevenimaginedyet

poly   amorous   verse
many   pome-making   tongue-entwined   langue
                                   leg-entwined

a new writing

a new writhing
a new exciting
a new inviting
a new delighting   language
               tongue   languishing
                       languid
               body   sandwiching
                               cultural way uv be-ing.   nod a pidgin
                                                           nod a dialect
uh hole new weigh uv   being with each other
                          speaking to each other
                          living with each other

       neurodiversit Y
makes   Grammuh   C.
insists on   Grammuh   C.
demands   Grammuh   C.
a revolution for   Grammuh   C.
                            Grammuh C eliminates   racism
                                           patriarchy
                                                 ableism
                                                 hegemony
                                                 classism
                                                 institutions
                                                 heterosexism
                                                 capitalism
                                                 all da udder isms.

fuck yo Grammar A.
we gon bury dat shit.
cuz "all alphabets are prisons" (Z. Richter, personal communication, March 27, 2014).

neurodiversity
makes   GrammarC.

◆ ◆ ◆

Impossibly, References

Le Guin, U. (1995). *Four ways to forgiveness.* NY: HarperPrism.

Weathers, W. (1980). *An alternate style: Options in composition.* Rochelle Park, NJ: Hayden Book Co.

❖   ❖   ❖

Chapter 10: Contrab(l)ooshuns to ecojustice from a dis{co}/inter/ruptive per[trans]formative maaaad studies

I'm uh   white
                male-presenting
                middle-class
                teacherlearneracademic.

                                    i identify as being disabled.
                                    I also identify as being mad, but hopefully not at
                                    you. And neurodivergent. And neuroqueer (which is
                                    as much a verb as it is a noun).

Lotsa folks say I'm   Crazy.
                       Batty.
                       Deranged.
                       Berserk.
                       Loony.
                       Dotty.
                       Insane.
                       Psycho.
                       Nuts.
                       Whacked.
                       Mad, so the saying goes, as a hatter.

The thing I am even has a number: 296.3.
I've always wanted to be a number.

many      mebbe most

                human people in the Eurocentric North
                have come to think

"...that the universe is made
up of very simple, clearly and
distinctly knowable things"
(Rorty, 1997, p. 357).

see, but it snot (er, ick):

the wired|weird|whirled|word|world is complex, messy, socio-culturally constructervated,
with multiple truths, and always already inherently ideological (Smith, 1999). more: if we
want to describe the world, we need—we must—reflect [ingpoollikea mirror] that complex/
messy/multiple/constructed/ideological nature in our stow reez.

i do that by calling on a complexifying performative poetics.

that means i act out a lot (thanks Utah one more time)

I speak/write/writhe in   ways
                                 weighs
                                          and means
that don't always make   immediate
                                 or mebbe N. E.
                                          cents to folks around me.

therefore.
to wit.
forthwith.

disa hillbill itybitty stud tease is the study of disability.

it is also, in part, about understanding how ableism works.

ableism is the systemic, institoot anal eyes ed social process of opera ression|session of disabled
people.

mad studies comes, sorta out of disability studies.

maaaaaad stud tease is, in parterated, about madness (the socially constructed state of being
crazy, or nutso).

mad studies   reclaims
              declaims
              enflames
                        madness as an identitooty.

mad studies is, in part, about understanding how saneism works.

saneism is the   systematic

automatic

conflagatory   in/out stitchintimesaves9 u{genic} shun alized Oprah(allie

allie)rah {de}pression of mad people. saneism is the thing that   enforces

reinforces

controls

the neuro**fuckinggoddam**typical in our kulchuh.

mad studies is alzo aroondandaboot working AGAINST saneism – mad studies is an activist thing as well as an acadoomic thing.

in our saneist Sandinista[not] kulchuh   linearity

rationality

sense

reason are dominate ate ate ing.

anything outside the board hers of the land of neuroNEROtypical is, by definition, mad.

mad studies is about opening up a plaize for people who are mad.

mad people are   non-linear

irrational

nonsensical

unreasonable

in our saneist culture.

in our professional discourse.

in ecojustice.

ecojustice education is a responze to a   "…dualism between social justice education and environmental education [and] is a reaction of a deeply rooted cultural problem that hyper-separates humans from the more than human world and promotes the general idea that humans have the right to manage, exploit, and control both other creatures and 'other' humans" (Lowenstein, Martusewicz, & Voelker, 2010, p. 101).

opposeratinging this dualism|schism iz

"an emerging framework for analyzing the deep cultural roots of and intersections within social and ecological violence, EcoJustice Education analyzes the destructive effects of a worldview organized by a logic of domination, and offers teachers and students ways of responding in their own communities" (Lowenstein, Martusewicz, & Voelker, 2010, p. 101).

It is also   "...a critical cultural and linguistic analysis
                    of the ecological and social crises—as inextricably
                    linked—through a critique of modernism, local-
                    global and scientific-technological perspectives, and
                    the mechanistic nature of root metaphors that frame
                    language and perception" (Kulnieks & Young, 2014,
                    p. 183).

doing disability studies/mad studies/ecojustice education requires us to be intersectional.
doing disability studies/mad studies/ecojustice education requires us to be interdisciplinary.
doing disability studies/mad studies/ecojustice education requires us to be ANTIdisciplinary.
doing that kind of work requires us to avoid simplicity.
to embrace complexity.
instead of working to simplify, we need to work to complexify.

So this thing that I'm doing here:
it is not a simple thing. it is opposed to simplicity.
it is not a linear thing. it is opposed to linearity.
it is not a rational thing. it is opposed to the rational.
it is not a reasonable thing. it is opposed to reason.
it is not a sensible thing. it rejoices in nonsense.

this performed poetic text will seek to complexify the shit outta some shit.
it will be an example of what a   possible
                                      complex
                                      irrational

                                   non-linear
                                   unreasonable
                                   nonsensical
                                   anti-ableist
                                   anti-saneist   discourse within ecojustice might start to
                                                   look like.
it will be, by definition, rooted in performative poetics.

what will be going on here and there and everywhere might not make $or¢ to you.
don't worry about it.
it won't bite you, or at least it won't bite you **hard**.
one way to work with this stuff is to try not to understand it.
let it wash over you, like the wind stirring in the trees.
or looking at a sculpture by Duchamp.
or listening to the music of John Cage.

ecojustice iz nod innocent.
its early bee ginmill ingswings are implicated in deep bad juju.
the early conservation movement was intrinsically tied to eugenics   (Allen, 2013; Corry,
                                                                       2015; Spiro, 2009;
                                                                       Wohlforth, 2010).
in fact (not fiction) the two things were inseparable
                                  attached at the crip hip
                                  not different from one another
        "eugenics and conservation were born twins" (Corry, 2015, n.p.).

in case you've forgotten, eugenics is also called social darwinism
        the word eugenics was invented
        in fact
        by the cousin of Charles Darwin
        a nice fella by the name of Francis Galton.
    eugenics is that happy little pseudo-scientific ideology
    created by the   Barbie™ and Ken™
                      white

patriarchal (apple pie) upper-crust
that brought you

- the creation and quantification of so-called intellectual disability and mental health;

- the often forgotten and ignored (at least by neurotypical and able-bodied folks) disability holocaust that murdered perhaps half a million disabled people in europe, wiped out an entire generation of Deaf people there, and served literally as the cultural and technical proving grounds for the larger and wider holocaust—all taught to the Nazis by the enterprising white upper-class scientific patriarchal elite of the United States;

- the forced sterilization of 70,000 impoverished disabled folks, women, indigenous people, and folks of color here in the United States, and a whole bunch more, globally;

- the creation of special education, a rampant eugenicist project that continues—to this day—to torture, segregate, and deny human and civil rights in the field of education to people with disabilities, indigenous peoples and other racial and ethnic minorities, and which had important, terrifying beginnings over 100 years ago in the university at which I'm employed.

eugenics, which remoons uvda day a   central
                                            foundational enterprise of (BIG WORD ALERT!)
                                            hegemonic
                               Eurocentric
                               Western
                               modernist
                               Cartesian
                               positivist
                               Northern
                               colonialist
                               racist
                               ableist

saneist
patriarchal   thought and culture—is an ideology, an
              entrenched system of ideas, and which,
              instead of disappearing many decades ago as
              most of us think, is extraordinarily pervasive
              in education and elsewhere to the present
              moment.

eugenics and the environmental justice movement are closely
                                                     tightly linked
                                                        woven
                                                     interconnected
early conservationists   "saw common ground between the destruction of America's flora
                           and fauna and the genetic decline of the Nordics"
and that   "Nordics were better suited to taming the wilderness while their
                           genetic inferiors seemed to thrive in 'the cramped factory and
                           crowded city'" (O'Reilly, 2013, n.p.)

just as|justice|just us disability studies has been criticized as being

disability studies, the movement for ecojustice education runs the risk of being a   white
                                                                                      ableist
                                                                                      saneist
ecojustice education movement   safely housed within middle and upper class boundaries
                                                                        (Wholforth, 2010),
                                  beholden to colonialist (Corry, 2015),
                                  and settler colonialist, ideologies.

the tiny and huge storeez we (Ma)tell® about environmental just-us and eduKAT(E)scion run
an enormous risk of being told   by

                              from the   totally privileged
                              white
                              dominant minority,
surrounded by (but still totally dominating) the   grassrooted
                                      margined
                                      edged
                                      boundaried
                                      segregated   majority.

the bodymind (~~not body and mind separate, binary~~, but one single thing) see, is a struggle for
meaning (McLaren & Leonardo, 1998). it is a struggle that must include at the very least a
revolutionary critical theory as yet unspoken outside of rancorous unreasonable pockets of
insurrection like the one happening on this page right now.
most stories told about people with disabilities—including most of those within and from
ecojustice—are owned and controlled by neurotypical and saneist professionals.
stow reeces peanut butter cups about disabled people can no longer be sung in   normalizing
                                                                         frame-locked
                                                                         bullshit
                                                                         vacademic
                                                                         language.
the lange guage of stand up sit down ardizing   acaredeemia
                                                        (its like a disease)
reinforces the armor-plated razor-wired bored hers de---signed to keep out themarginalia.
jargonate|jargonaut herdwords are used to create territorialization of knowledge about
        disability
        madness
        race
        gender
        class
dis lange assuage protects privileged   under
                                            over   standings {vinyl} residing
in the landseaair escapes of the acayuckademy from infection by viral ebola in/outbreaks of

        radical
        critical
        anti-normalized   thought.

dis   perfomerated
        excommunicated   writhing writing   enters hear
                                                       (exit only)
from   "the spring of the imagination,
        when the winter of clean positivism
        fades completely and we are fre/er/iere"
        (Zach Richter, personal communication, April 25, 2013).
accept, of course, positivism wud never clean, not even by the Tide® laundry detergent of
manufactured epissed em offl ogical ocean of Comte and his followers
               (and, for good measure, fuck you Foucault)
               (I've been waiting years to write that line).
It is   embodied
        and imbedded
        and has been bedded   (a beast wid 2 approxiMATE backs)
        and lived   to tell
                    the tall
                    tell-tail
                    tale
                    tee(hee) beer
in the reel live bawdy bodies
of reel live   plant and
               rock and
               soil and
               animal and
               water and
               human   peoples and in terrupt/terrogate the world.
Here, I always already critique the creation
                          consumption
                          cooption
                          commercialization

                          commodification
                          consorbtion
of   universalist
         eugenicist
         monocultural   e ducat scion from the place of the   counter-hegemonic
                                                                              neurodiverse
                                                                              queer
                                                                              polyculture.

be caw caw cawz   the planet and its rock/plant/water/soil/animal/human peoples are
                          bee ying

destroyed
de-storied
de lang waged.

witch just ain't good enough.
nod fer da crips and queers dat I hang wid. me and mine(d).
my homies in da neurodiver[ticulosis]gent (should be femme) activism and scholarship
thingie claim their
              our   right to be who   they
                                      we   are and who   they
                                                            we want to be in a
not-yet-our-culture-because-it-hasn't-entirely-been-created-or-imagined.
we're queer gonna mage our way into a new corpogoddamnreality that rejects da
              pure-snow-white
              honkey
              strait
              straight
              bourgeois
              subdude

BORING

whatever you wanna call what it is we got now.
FUCK that shit.

        anarchoneuroqueer
        crazy-as-a-motherfucker   and owning
                     celebrating
                     claiming   shit.

and through that ownership/celebration/claiming, creating a radical youtopia(ry)n vision
(deaf and) of what will cum.
I have absofuckinglutely no ideer (in da headlights) what this   space
                                (the final frunteer)

looks like or smells like or tastes like or how to make it happenin', Jackson.
only that it needs to.
and that it needs to be created by and for and with   neurodivergent
                                   mad
                                   disabled
                                   neuroanarchoqueer
rock/plant/water/animal/human peep (hole) coa lishons.
but the cool (totally frigid[aire]) thingking is, see, that eye donerated half (or three-quarters)
to   know
        sow
        blow
        GO!
                what it loogs lige, matey.
this is not some kinda hocus pocus locus,
hear me out and back in the screen door of somnambulant justusice, nossuh;
its not some weird
                wired
                whored
                word buncha (prolly pot, huh) smoke and freak show mirrors (here's lookin' at
you, kid).
the abolootionists didn't have a clew (sailing along) what an Amurrican   soziety
                                               coquettery

without slavery would look like, only that slavery must end.
they made it up as they went along (Ben-Moshe, 2012).

wee can do da zame.

when we've finisherated, if we ged id (w)right, whether we're (w)rong or right, whether we're wroing, we won't even have to conceeve of

> the
> strange
> cool
> ting
> we call
> ecojustice.

it'll be that fucking cool, hey?

♦   ♦   ♦

References

Allen, G. (2013). "Culling the herd': Eugenics and the conservation movement in the United States, 1900-1940. *Journal of the History of Biology, 46*(1), 31-72. doi: 10.1007/s10739-011-9317-1.

Ben-Moshe, L. (2012). Towards abolition of the carceral: Lessons from deinstitutionalization and prison abolition. Annual Conference of the Society of Disability Studies, Denver, CO.

Corry, S. (2015). The colonial origins of conservation: The disturbing history behind US national
parks. *Truthout*. Retrieved from http://www.truth-out.org/opinion/item/32487-the-colonial-origins-of-conservation-the-disturbing-history-behind-us-national-parks

Kulnieks, A. & Young, K. (2014). Literacies, leadership, and inclusive education: Socially just arts-informed eco-justice pedagogy. *LEARNing Landscapes, 7*(2), 183-192.

Lowenstein, E., Martusewicz, R., & Voelker, L. (2010). Developing teachers' capacity for ecojustice education and community-based learning. *Teacher Education Quarterly, 37*(4), 99-118.

O'Reilly, E. (2013). Redwoods and Hitler: The link between nature conservation and the eugenics movement. New-York Historical Society blog From The Stacks blog. Retrieved from http://blog.nyhistory.org/redwoods-and-hitler-the-link-between-nature-conservation-and-the-eugenics-movement/

Smith, P. (1999). Drawing new maps: A radical cartography of developmental disabilities. *Review of Educational Research, 69* (2), 117-144.

Spiro, J. (2009). *Defending the master race: Conservation, eugenics, and the legacy of Madison Grant*. Burlington: University of Vermont Press.

Wohlforth, C. (2010). Conservation and eugenics. Orion, 28. Retrieved from https://orionmagazine.org/article/conservation-and-eugenics/

Chapter 11: An Immoderate Maaaaaadness: Why We're Pissed, What We're Gonna Do About It, and Why We're Not Asking Your Permission[7]

Trigger Warning for profanity and a complete lack of, or more properly a pronounced disregard for, propriety and general social decorum. Cuz, dat's how i

roll
role
stroll
patrol
prowl
flow

i don't know what   i'm   doing.
i don't know what   i'm   doing.
i don't know wha   thyme dew wing.
i don't no whud   i'm   da wang.

there is a certain amount of (heisenberg) uncertainty here.

in this text are a certain number of   planned
     un planned
     planed
     un planed
     rough
     smooth

---

[7] With special thanks to my co-conspiratorial accomplices Kira Dallaire, Lzz Johnk, Rachel Lewandowksi, and Jacquie St. Antoine.

inter[n] **text**ual

inter	sexual	(viva la revolucion!)
inter	processual	
inter	lexical	
inter	lanoitceric	
in	fernal	
coffee	liqueur	
rocket	larkspur	
inter	perpetual	(on and on and on and on and on....)

(non)connections.

count them.

one two three four five six seven eight nine ten eleven twelve thirteen fourteen fifteen

don't tri 2 make sensce of dis. let id mage scents uv ewe.

repetition
repetition
repetition
repetition
repetition
repetition
repetition
repetition

dishabille stud tease iz uh   thing.
                               ding a ling.
it didn't usta bee uh thing.
be4 it wuz uh thing, there were   other things.
                               udder tings.

utter   tings pings strings wings thrings clings
utterings.
mutterings.

those   other things   were
                                   made   or
                                   done   or
                                   seen   or
                                   heard   or
                                   said   or
                                   written or

known by
people who didn't identify as being disabled.

becuz disabled people couldn't possibly   know   things.
becuz disabled people couldn't possibly   write   things.
becuz disabled people couldn't possibly   say   things.
becuz disabled people couldn't possibly   hear   things.
becuz disabled people couldn't possibly   see   things.
becuz disabled people couldn't possibly   do   things.
becuz disabled people couldn't possibly   make   things.

wry cud dunt deshabilled pebblepeeple pause ebly
                                   makedoseehearsaywriteknow   things?
because people who didn't identify as being disabled said they couldn't.

people who didn't identify as being disabled were, and are, in control.
people who didn't identify as being disabled were, and are, in charge.
people who didn't identify as being disabled were, and are, in power.
people who didn't identify as being disabled had, and have, privilege.
people who didn't identify as being disabled have, and do, control the shots.
people who didn't identify as being disabled have, and do, dominate.
people who didn't identify as being disabled have, and do, rule.

they werearehadhavedo   controlchargepowerprivilegecontroltheshotsdominaterule because
of ableizm, which is another thing, which is an   ideology.
                                                      video logic.
                                                      idiot logic.
uv middle-upper cishet white settler-colonialist neoliberal dead guys

i don't know what i'm doing.

this here is mysterious scholarship, a scholarship of mystery. a scholarship that cannot be
     cited
     referenced
     peer-reviewed
     tenure-tracked
     CV-ed
     published
     presented
     put in conference proceedings

          this   scholarship
     scow lower ship
     sloop upper boat
     cannod bee pain   ted
                         ed
                         fred
                         ned
                         dead
     in da ideology uv ableizm.
cuz, dontcha know, ableizt ideology is caught up in the   meaning-making
                                                                  meaning-receiving
                                                                  world defining

     structures of the   dominant
                           da mine ant
                                     dominating
                           da mine ant hating

hegemony
hedge fund $

i don't know what i'm doing.

Maaaaaaaaadness.
Maaaaaaaaadness.

Mad studies   is a thing.
Mad stud tease   is a thing.
it deednut usta buzzbee uh   tingaling.
                                    dingaling.
                                    dangling.   frumm da ledge of cccrrraaaaaaaaaaaazzzyyy
                                    wrangling.   frumm da ledge of cccrrraaaaaaaaaaaazzzyyy
                                    mangling.   frumm da ledge of cccrrraaaaaaaaaaaazzzyyy
                                    tangling.   frumm da ledge of cccrrraaaaaaaaaaaazzzyyy
                                    jangling.   frumm da ledge of cccrrraaaaaaaaaaaazzzyyy

Mad studies is a good thing,   2.   4 6 8 who do we appreciate?
Mad studies is an important thing,   2.
Mad studies is a real thing,   2.

discursive (inter)(dis)(e)(cor)ruption.
jamming with/jamming the enjambment.

repetition.
repetition.
repetition.
repetition.
repetition.
repetition.
repetition.

fission clinician cognition emission competition sedition suspicion
there is a certain amount of uncertainty here.

then disability studies became a thing.
disabled people made it a thing.
disabled people wanted to make decisions about what disability studies was.
disabled people wanted to make decisions about what disability studies involves.
disabled people wanted to make decisions about what disability studies research and scholarship
entails.
because disability studies is about disabled people.
and disability studies is about understanding ableizm.

Mad studies is a thing about madness; a thing about crazy and psychiatric disabilities and
emotional disabilities and behavioral disabilities.
Mad studies didn't used to be a thing. Before mad activism and mad studies were things, there
were   other   things.

uvver tings.
covertings. (making covert, hidden, excluded)
covortings (dancing, romping, loud fun)

Those other things were made

or   done
or   seen
or   said
or   heard
or   written
or   known

by people who didn't identify as being mad.

Because, they said

mad people couldn't possibly know things.

Because, they said

mad people couldn't possibly write things.

Because, they said

mad people couldn't possibly say things.

Because, they said

mad people couldn't possibly hear things.

Because, they said

mad people couldn't possibly see things.

Because, they said

mad people couldn't possibly do things.

Because, they said

mad people couldn't possibly make things.

Why did they say that **mad people** couldn't possibly

make/do/see/hear/say/write/know things?

Because people who didn't identify as being mad said they couldn't, that's why, dude.

Because of saneism. Which is another   ideo   logy
                                               idiot   logic

which pissed **mad people**   off.
                      real   off.
                         they got   mad.
                             REAL mad.

Disabled people began to understand that, for too long, they have been

segregated   captivated   castrated   mistreated
        harvested   dominated   annihilated   liquidated
            eradicated   intimidated   discriminated   muted
                convicted   exterminated   accosted
                    hated   detested   experimented
                        addlepated   ejected   insulted
                            executed   abducted
                                decapitated   humiliated
                                    maltreated

and

euthanized
pathologized
hypnotized
chastised
sterilized
categorized
jeopardized

disorganized
supervised
hospitalized
disenfranchised
scrutinized
immobilized
traumatized
impersonalized
compromised
generalized
misadvised

                              hysterectomized
                        excised
                        tranquillized
                        ghettoized
                        victimized
                        analyzed
                        lobotomized
                        colonized
                        neutralized
                        sentimentalized
                        pauperized
                        ostracized
                        satirized
                        minimized
                        victimized
                        dehumanized
                        narcotized
                        containerized
                        stigmatized
                        homogenized
                        sterilized
                        brutalized
                        neutralized
                        anesthetized
                        criminalized
                        pulverized
                        desexualized
                        sanitized
                        institutionalized
                        patronized

and and and and and and and and and and and

thing.

then mad studies became a

mad people
made it a thing.

mad people
wanted to make decisions about what mad studies was.

mad people
wanted to make decisions about what mad studies involves.

mad people
wanted to make decisions about what mad studies research and scholarship entails.

because
and this is really important—
mad studies

is about
mad people. (I know. who knew?)

and mad studies
is about understanding saneizm.

Mad people began to understand that, for too long, they have been
labeled
culled
swindled

hassled
strangled
bamboozled
trampled
cudgled
gulled
annulled
sizzled
cancelled
baffled
pommeled
crumpled

and and and and and and and and and and and

kept

                                                                out

forced

                                                                out

of the common homespun fabric of   MODERNIST

                                      CARTESIAN

                                      PATRIARCHAL

                                      WESTERN

                                      NORTHERN

                                      WHITE

                                      EUROCENTRIC culture.

repetition
repetition
repetition
repetition
repetition
repetition
repetition
repetition

Their oppression and discrimination has been at the hands and
    minds and
    legs and
    eyes and
    ears

and and and and and and and and **and and and**

of walking talking hearing   seeing
    logical
    coherent
    rational
    linear
    sensible
    lucid
    reasonable

neuro**fuckinggoddam**typical

colonizing
neoliberal
racist

cishet

ableist   zo   zi   eh   tee

        intent on ensuring the dominance of that   stinking

testosterone-poisoned prevailing hegemony

through the deployment of a professionalized eugenicizt Rmee of culljure powlice that batrol

the bobwhah fenzes that enclothe and project the   high

and mighty academicohsoconveniently **white** ivorytowers of

special educa shun

rehabilitat   shun

therapew   pewpewpew

tic(k) crawling up our legs to infect us all with some damn ableist lyme disease aversive

disciplined and protected and sanctioned by the overlord bosses uv neocon 'murricuh.

(can I have an amen? can I have an halleluiah?)

i don't know what i'm doing.

really.

disability studies has an ideology too.

the ideology of disability studies

is

a   complex

        intersectional

        antidisciplinary

        gnu

        post-post waive uv

        anti   hierarchic

        counter   institutional

        oppositional defiance

For too long, medical-model eugenicizt professionals have controlled disability research. Disabled people need to create, control, and enact disability research and scholarship projects about disability.

Mad people need to create, control, and enact research and scholarship projects about madness. People who identify as being mad need to create, control, and enact research and scholarship projects about mad studies. mad studies needs to be accountable to the needs, wants, dreams, and desires of mad people.

stop appropriating our
>   minds
>   bodies
>   bodyminds
>   souls

in the service of your
>   career
>   reputation
>   tenure

especially if we don't even get a paycheck or get to choose where we live or even decide if we GET to live.

fuck your goddam dominating colonizing prevailing ablest hegemony.
we're gonna bury DAT shit.

>   there is no conclusion to this wry thing.
>   there is no conclusion to this revolution.

>   this is not a request.
>   we aren't asking.
>   we aren't saying please.

fish or cut bait.
stay or go home.
shit or get off the pot.
be with us or get the out of the way.

About the Author

Phil Smith is, in a nutshell, post-everything—he is SO after that. He's a big-deal perfesser guy at Eastern Michigan University, where he slips disability studies stuff and the occasional cranky rants into courses he teaches, and hopes the bureaucraps and curricula police won't notice. He's also the director of the Brehm Center for Special Education Scholarship and Research. Phil received the Emerging Scholar Award in Disability Studies in Education in 2009, and EMU's College of Education Innovative Scholarship Award in 2015. He's had papers published in a buncha journals, as well as a lotta book chapters, been on several journal review boards, and presented at so many conferences he's given up counting. He's published two books in the Peter Lang Disability Studies in Education series, *Whatever Happened to Inclusion? The Place of Students with Intellectual Disabilities in Education* and *Both Sides of the Table: Autoethnographies of Educators Learning and Teaching With/In [Dis]ability,* and edited a textbook entitled, *Disability and Diversity: An Introduction.* He's a published poet, playwright, novelist, and visual and performance artist, and izza critical scholar and a whatever-comes-after-qualitative researcher. For more than 25 years, in a variety of contexts and roles, he has worked as a disability rights activist, and served on the boards of directors of a number of international, regional, state, and local organizations, including as President of the Society for Disability Studies. He's mad (but not, mostly, angry) as hell, and identifies as disabled. He rides his bicycle a lot, and tries to remember to wear his socks. A transplanted Yankee, he makes maple syrup at Flamingo Farm, and spends as much time as he can beside Lake Superior, where loons, wolves, moose, and bald eagles peek in the windows of his cabin.

About the Cover Artist

Jacqueline Pruder St. Antoine is a mother, a mad person, a wife, a reader and writer, a mad studies and disability studies scholar, an artist and performer, a student and teacher, a lover of artichokes and dinosaurs, a wannabe gardener. She works to bring a mad studies perspective to new spaces and investigate new ways of being, understanding, and representing research, feelings, and knowledge. Jacquie aims to make her work arts-based and performative in nature, accessible, and emotive… exploring the nuances of madness, disability, and what it means to exist in an ableist, saneist multi-verse.

Made in the USA
Middletown, DE
06 September 2018